Children: Child Care

David M. Houghton
and
Mary C. McColgan

Published by
Collins Educational Ltd
77–85 Fulham Palace Road
Hammersmith
London
W6 8JB

First Published 1995

British Cataloguing in Publication Data is
available from the British Library.

ISBN 0–00–322334–5

This book is dedicated to:
Benjamin, Deborah, Josephine,
Michael, Rachael, Rebecca and Timothy (DMH);
and my mother, Teresa, and children Aoife and Aodhan (MCMcC).

Typeset by Harper Phototypesetters Limited, Northampton, England
Cover design by Wheeler and Porter
Printed in Great Britain by Scotprint, Musselburgh

Contents

Acknowledgements		**v**
Introduction		**vi**
Section 1 Beginning work with children *David M. Houghton*		
1	Attachment to parents and separation	**1**
2	The emergence of a self-identity	**11**
3	Children's gender awareness	**19**
Section 2 Promoting children's social and emotional development *David M. Houghton*		
4	Children's socialization	**27**
5	Understanding and alleviating children's anxieties	**36**
6	Aggressive children	**45**
7	Right and wrong and children	**54**
Section 3 Observing and assessing children *David M. Houghton*		
8	Communicating with children	**63**
9	Observing, recording and assessing	**72**
10	Watching children play	**82**
Section 4 Partnership and child-focused protection *Mary C. McColgan*		
11	Partnership with parents	**94**
12	Team membership and teamwork	**105**
13	Protecting children	**113**
14	Empowerment and anti-oppressive practice	**125**
References		**134**
Index		**137**

Titles available in the
Working with People Series

Coordinating Care at Home
Tim Dant and Val Gully

Introducing Community Care
Peter Sharkey

Skilled Work with People
Robert Adams

Working with Children
David Houghton and Mary McColgan

Acknowledgements

The authors would like to thank Jo Campling for persuading them to write this book and the Series Editor, Robert Adams, who helped them to keep their writing grounded in practice and who was a constant source of encouragement.

They also wish to express their gratitude to Patrick McNeill of HarperCollins Publishers whose rigorous attention to detail and efficient management of the drafts they submitted was an invaluable support. Thanks are due also to Maude Kelly who patiently deciphered Mary McColgan's handwriting and who carefully typed her chapters; and to David Houghton's old and well-worn word processor for seeing him through yet another mammoth exercise.

The publisher and the author would also like to thank the following:

Chatto and Windus for permission to reproduce an extract from *Separation: Anxiety and Anger* in The Attachment and Loss trilogy (Bowlby, 1975).

Macmillan Press Ltd for permission to reproduce an extract from *Social Development in Early Childhood* (Schaffer, 1981).

Tavistock Publications for permission to reproduce an extract from *The Making and Breaking of Affectional Bonds* (Bowlby, 1979).

Yale University Press for permission to reproduce an extract from *Becoming: Basic Consideration for a Psychology of Personality* (Allport, 1955).

The extract from 'Early Social Development' by H.R. Schaffer in Slater, A. and Bremner, J.G. (eds) *Infant Development* is reprinted by permission of Lawrence Erlbaum Associates Ltd., Hove, UK.

Introduction

A number of influences prompted the emergence of this book. It is intended to meet the needs of those who wish to forge a stronger link between broadening their knowledge and sharpening their practical competence when working with children. It should be helpful to those seeking National Vocational Qualifications in Child Care and Education who wish to underpin their practice with relevant knowledge. The practical exercises may be included in a portfolio for purposes of assessment.

The contents of the book have been drawn largely from the authors' experiences in teaching a course in child development, education and care at the University of Ulster. The course was introduced by David Houghton in 1989 because he believed that a well-trained early years' workforce could contribute to the mental health of children and their families. It also emphasizes the importance of integrating care with education in both training and providing for young children. It was the first course of its kind in the UK to provide a university education and training for mature students who had not received special training for their work with young children. Universities in Britain are now introducing similar degree courses.

The wealth of experience with children which the students have brought to the course has acted as a touchstone for both the relevance and practical value of its content. The information contained in each chapter within this book and most of the related practical exercises were tried and evaluated by those students. The authors are indebted to them for that contribution. The book is divided into sections which reflect the fundamental concerns of early years' workers: beginning work with children, promoting children's social and emotional development, observing and assessing children, partnership and child-focused protection.

Throughout this book, children come first. Evidence from medicine and psychology indicates that at no other time during the human life span is the rate of physical and mental growth as fast as during the early years of childhood. This, together with the fact that children have no say in whether they are born into this world, means that the responsibility is on adults in particular, whether as parents or professional carers, and on societies in general to offer the best care to the world's children.

The long overdue recognition of children's rights in European legislation and in the UK's Children Act (1989) affirms this obligation. It reinforces the view that children should have their thoughts and feelings acknowledged and acted upon for their benefit. These should be recognized in meeting their right to protection.

The contents of each chapter and the practical exercises are intended to encourage readers to develop an ongoing analysis and reflection of their work with children through an effective, close interaction with them. Perhaps the most effective tutors for the improvement of our professional practice are the children themselves.

1

Attachment to parents and separation

Preview

What is the nature of the relationship between children and their parents? How might the relationship affect children's immediate and long-term future? This chapter examines:

- the attachment relationship;
- the quality of caring that leads to children's feelings of security;
- how children might react to short- and long-term separations from their parents.

Relationships between children and parents

In any decision about children's best interests, how they attach to their parents is an overriding consideration. This relationship must be taken into account by anyone providing for children's care and education.

Most work with children is concerned with how the link between children and their parents influences the children's lives. The separation of children from their parents, whether forced or voluntary, is always an important issue. The professional and public debate about the strengths and effects of child–parent bonds is neverending.

The opinions of experts and the findings of research into this topic are sought by those who have to make decisions about children's lives. The paramount concern of child-care policy, practice and legislation is to guard and promote that which protects children's welfare – that is their physical, psychological and social well-being. Judges, social workers, psychologists, teachers, child-care workers – indeed, parents themselves – all need to know the importance of the relationships between a child and her or his parents for that child's future.

> Many principles and practices for working with families are based on the belief that the bond between children and their parents influences not only children's present wellbeing but also their future lives as adults.

A child–parent relationship starts with a baby's first gasp of breath. This relationship fascinates and puzzles those who work with families. Some say the infant–parent bond determines a person's life into and throughout adulthood, although others disagree.

What are these beliefs based on? If we want to understand how we might best care for and educate children, we need to start at the beginning. From the moment of their entry into the world, children start to make demands upon others. Babies cry to let their parents or other carers know that they need to be fed, changed, reassured and cuddled: they need attention. In turn, parents make demands upon their infant children: 'Wait a minute while I take the pan off the heat,' 'Lie still so that I can put your nappy on,' 'Hang on until your feed cools' . . . and so on.

Some experts consider the dependent relationships which develop between children and their parents to be nature's way of making sure that the young learn to cope with the task of living. In the animal kingdom, the focus of parenting is to enable the young to become increasingly independent, to be able eventually to survive without their parents' constant support.

Beginnings of attachment

John Bowlby, a British psychiatrist, and Mary Ainsworth, an American psychologist who worked with Bowlby in London during the early 1950s, have had a considerable influence on what we believe about attachments between children and parents. Work with delinquent boys and children who were homeless after World War Two had confirmed Bowlby's view:

> What is believed to be essential for mental health is that the infant and young child should experience a warm, intimate and continuous relationship with his mother (or permanent mother substitute) in which both find satisfaction and enjoyment.
>
> (Bowlby 1975, p.11)

Learning about attachment from observing animals

Imprinting

Bowlby's ideas about the attachment between a mother and her child were very much influenced by the findings of ethologists, who studied the behaviour of animals in their normal environment. In 1951, Sir Julian Huxley, a British biologist, introduced Bowlby to research by Niko Tinbergen and that of Konrad Lorenz in the 1930s.

Lorenz and Tinbergen were interested in the bonding behaviours which existed between young animals and their mothers, and in the patterns of behaviours that had not been learned but appeared to be inborn. Writing in 1935, Lorenz noticed that newly-born ducklings and goslings followed whatever was in their immediate vicinity. He called this 'imprinting'.

In 1970 Sluckin, a psychologist who had also studied these animal behaviours, described their characteristics. Anyone who works with young children will instantly recognize these as behaviours which they meet all the time in helping children settle in their crèche, playgroup or nursery class. He broke down these behaviours into five distinct elements.

1 Distress at separation. Distress calls are made when infants are separated from that to which they are attached.
2 Recognition at reunion. The figure imprinted upon them (usually a parent) is more readily approached and followed.
3 Choice of the familiar. Infants prefer people with whom they are familiar to those who may be less familiar.

4 Running to mother. Infants will try to keep close to the figure they are attached to and will move towards that person if confronted by a strange figure.
5 Work for a reunion. If infants are at a distance from, or cannot see, the imprinted figure, they will work hard at overcoming any obstacle to be reunited with their 'parent' figure.

Sensitive periods

Lorenz and Sluckin found that infant animal attempts at attachment to a carer were most successful if they happened within a particular period (from a few hours up to a day or two) after birth. Lorenz called this time the **critical period**. Sluckin referred to it as the **sensitive period**.

Sluckin wanted to emphasize that, although the quality of the relationship between the newborn and a carer might be much affected by their contact within a particular period of time, the relationship could also be influenced by later circumstances. His view of the sensitive period as being the best – but not the only – time for particular behaviours to develop gives more hope of success to adopting and fostering parents than extreme views about critical periods for bonding.

Some psychologists and educationalists believe that there are similar sensitive periods throughout human development. They try to identify when these might be and what form they might take for the processes involved in, for example, learning to read and in becoming numerate, and in developing other life skills.

Bonding between mother and child

In his studies of human families, Bowlby claimed that the sorts of attachment behaviours found among animals could also be found in human relationships. He claimed that many behaviours which appear to be instinctive in human infants – such as sucking, clinging and following – are for the purpose of keeping the mother near at hand to attend to the infant's needs and thereby ensure survival.

Bowlby said that during the first two years of life infants need to attach to one particular carer, usually their mother. In 1977, elaborating upon his ideas, Bowlby suggested that attachment is a life-long process:

> Whilst especially evident during early childhood, *attachment behaviour is held to characterize human beings from the cradle to the grave.*
>
> (1979, p.129, authors' emphasis)

Bowlby drew attention to the consequences of inadequate bonding. Children who did not benefit from a mother's 'warm, intimate and continuous relationship' were considered by Bowlby to be suffering from **maternal deprivation**. He maintained that a child can be deprived even when living at home if her or his mother fails to give the child necessary loving care. On the other hand, a person other than a child's mother – whom the child knows and trusts – can provide a substitute. But in both these cases, Bowlby would consider the child to suffer **partial deprivation**. A child with no close, secure relationship at all suffered what he called **complete deprivation**.

Bowlby said that three variables influence the effects of deprivation:

1 the age at which a child loses a mother;
2 the length of time a child is separated from a mother;
3 the degree of deprivation a child experiences.

Bowlby pointed to sensitive or critical periods for infants. A child between six and 12 months of age might never recover from the effects of more than three months' deprivation.

Deprivation up to five years of age could have a serious consequence.

Separation from mother

In 1958, research by Harry Harlow in America seemed to support the importance of a close bond with a mother figure. He separated infant rhesus monkeys shortly after birth from their mothers and put them with 'surrogate' mothers; he substituted wire models for their real mothers. One model had a feeding bottle, the other was covered with sponge rubber and terry towelling.

All the infant monkeys became attached to the towelling mother, even those which had been fed by the other model. When frightened, they ran to the towelling mother. When she was absent, they were distressed and explored their surroundings far less. Harlow showed that infants attached because their mothers were a source of comfort, not because of 'cupboard love', and not because mothers provided food.

Young monkeys which were separated from their real mothers and attached to the surrogate mother, later showed signs of social and emotional problems. They were more timid and more easily bullied, paid little attention to the other monkeys and were aggressive when they were approached by them socially. They bit and wounded themselves. When they matured, they could not mate satisfactorily and the females proved to be inadequate mothers.

These animal studies provided evidence for Bowlby's claims about the consequences of maternal deprivation. He was certain that children benefited from secure attachments to their mothers. Bowlby thought that the benefits gained from secure attachments to mothers explained 'why children thrive better in bad homes than in good institutions, and why children with bad parents are, apparently unreasonably, so attached to them . . . ' (1953, p.78).

John Bowlby was very influential in the 1950s in directing opinions and policies about what we should strive for in child–parent relationships. Many policymakers and child-care workers claim to have based their decisions and actions upon his line of thinking, following his conclusion that any sort of natural mother is better than a surrogate because she provides the continuity of the initial attachment in infant–mother bonding.

A World Health Organization Expert Committee in 1951 considered that day nurseries and crèches gave rise to 'permanent damage to the emotional health of a future generation' (Clarke and Clarke, 1976, p.23). The same view sparked off debates about the outcomes of 'late' adoptions, and many other issues in child development.

Criticisms of Bowlby

As is often the case in scholarly research, there has been criticism of Bowlby's work. Some have criticised his viewpoint by questioning his evidence.

Bowlby emphasizes children's separation from parents. But the whole issue of the deprivation of children is much more complex than this, as Clarke and Clarke

(1976) point out. Many of the children in the research used by Bowlby to support his ideas were already in a state of deprivation when they were observed and continued in that state afterwards.

A more thorough-going investigation would need to know about a child's circumstances before and after a period of deprivation. It is important to know what sort of deprivation a child had suffered, whether it was emotional, social or a failure by carers to offer a stimulating environment to the child. Bowlby's evidence is inconclusive on these points.

> By experimental standards . . . the Maternal Deprivation Theory has no significant scientific support, and there is sufficient counter-evidence to make it decidedly improbable.
>
> (Morgan, 1975, p.18)

Parents' sensitivity to babies' needs

Mary Ainsworth left Bowlby's team in London to go to Uganda in 1954 with her husband. While there she spent time with Ganda families, watching how sensitive and responsive the mothers were towards their babies' needs. She noted the babies' attachment behaviours towards their mothers. Observing twenty-eight child-and-mother pairs, she noticed how the babies stopped crying when lifted by their mothers, but not when lifted by anyone else. They also smiled and 'talked' to their mothers but not usually to others.

> Ainsworth concluded that babies became secure, insecure or non-attached with their mothers, depending upon how sensitive and responsive to their needs the mothers had been.

At the Johns Hopkins University in Baltimore, USA, from 1963 to 1967, Mary Ainsworth continued her study of infants' attachment behaviours towards their mothers in the normal surroundings of their homes. She found the attachment behaviours of the American infants similar to those she had watched in Uganda. She compared how Ganda mothers kept their babies close by. If something had to be done somewhere else in the house, they took their babies with them. But when they worked in the garden, Ganda mothers left their babies for three or four hours. On the other hand, the middle-class Baltimore mothers tended more often to leave their babies in one room while they moved around rooms working – popping in and out to keep an eye on their babies.

> Babies in different cultures might react differently to their mothers leaving them, depending upon their previous experiences of separation.

The American infants could expect their mothers to call back in a few moments to check that all was well, but a Ganda infant had learned that when mother left she would be away, and out of reach for some hours. Not surprisingly, in their own homes, the American children did not seem too bothered when their mothers left them in a room; but the Ganda infants were much more upset by their mothers' departures.

This lack of concern by American infants when their mothers left them alone in a room meant that Ainsworth could not get any real clue as to which infants felt secure and which felt insecure. To overcome this she brought the children and their mothers into the university – an unfamiliar and strange situation for the children. She thought this would allow a clearer indication of the children's secure and insecure reactions when their mothers left them to go somewhere else.

Infants' reactions to strange situations

The method Ainsworth used is now widely known and used:

- The mother and baby were put in a room where the mother watched while her baby was given the opportunity to play with toys and to explore the room.
- A stranger then entered the room and after a minute talked with the mother for another minute.
- Then the stranger moved near to the baby and after a minute the mother left as unobtrusively as possible.
- The baby was left in the room with the stranger during which time the stranger fitted in with the baby's behaviours, joining in if the baby offered a toy, etc. (This session was stopped if the baby was very distressed.)
- The mother then returned to comfort her baby and to settle her or him down to play.
- When she left again, she waved goodbye, drawing attention to her departure.

In another episode, when the baby had been playing alone, a stranger entered and joined in the baby's activities. Mother then returned and lifted her baby into her arms as the stranger left. The whole session lasted about 25 minutes, three minutes for each of the episodes described.

On the basis of what she observed in these sessions, Ainsworth described the infants' reactions in one of three ways.

1. Secure infants were those for whom the mother clearly provided a secure base, who were at ease while the mother was at hand and, although they were upset when she left, they were soon consoled and settled when she returned.
2. Anxious-ambivalent infants were those who showed mixed reactions to the mother, clinging before separation but not always running or showing any clear sign of welcome when she returned.
3. Anxious-avoidant children did not approach the mother for comfort even when they were upset and did not react very anxiously to strangers.

During pre-school and primary school, children who had been secure as infants were found to be:

- more competent than their peers who had shown signs of anxious attachment as infants, and;
- more sensitive to relationships with peers and adults.

Changes in a mother's life influence the nature of her child's attachment to her. For example, when a single parent develops a secure relationship with a partner or a mother is relieved from pressing money worries, for example, their children also feel more secure.

Anxious-avoidant children try to establish a secure relationship with adults in their lives such as teachers or relatives, according to researches by Ainsworth's followers. They claim that parents of insecurely attached children mistake their child's negative behaviours as revealing a lack of love, when they are in fact a child's way of coping with puzzling relationships.

Questioning Ainsworth's studies

In fairness to children and their parents, and to our own attempts to understand relationships between children and their parents, we need to question the work of Ainsworth and her followers. Ainsworth-type observations might not give an accurate picture. What if the infant who makes no particular fuss when the mother returns feels perfectly secure and is not stressed but can cope with her leaving and returning because the bond is strong and not threatened by such events?

Perhaps infant reactions do not result from rearing but from inherited personality characteristics. Some children might be shy or irritable by nature, not because of attachment relationships with their parents.

Mothers' care for their children was assessed by how their children reacted when mothers left and returned a couple of times to a strange room. The quality of the mothers' caring was never directly observed in the natural environment of their home, as it was in Ainsworth's study of Ganda mothers. There has not been much follow-up research to check thoroughly on these claims, mainly because it would require a longitudinal study, studying the same children from infancy through to adolescence or beyond. This would be costly and time-consuming.

The importance of Ainsworth's work is its emphasis upon getting the relationship between children and their parents right. This acts as a counterbalance for approaches to child-rearing which emphasise practical techniques: potty training versus no training, bottle versus breast-feeding, demand feeding versus scheduled feeding, and so on.

Attachment and carers

Sensitive responsiveness to children's needs

When Shaffer and Emerson (1964) studied the first 18 months of life for 60 infants, they found that children in the home became attached to adults who were sensitively responsive to their needs. In about one third of the families, the children's main attachment was to a father, a close relative or a brother or sister, and not to the primary care-taker in the family.

In families with a few adults in them, children attached to more than one person, because more than one was sensitive to their needs. This was contrary to what Bowlby had suggested.

Others have pointed out that adverse consequences do not always result from a child's separation from a parent. It is the meaning of the separation from the child's point of view that influences how it affects that child.

Michael Rutter, a British psychiatrist, came to this conclusion in 1971. He had studied children separated because:

- their mothers were at work;
- they had experienced a number of mother figures caring for them, or;

- they had been in full-day care.

Rutter found that the quality of the family relationships affects the child more than the separation itself. For example, children separated because of disharmony between their parents are more likely to show the sorts of reaction described by Bowlby than children separated by the death of a parent. Rutter also discovered that although children between six months and four years of age who had been separated by short stays in hospital reacted in the ways Bowlby had predicted, being separated from their brothers and sisters also had this effect.

Young children were less distressed when their brothers and sisters accompanied them to hospital. Previous experience of staying in hospital also helped to lessen any negative reactions to separation. We need to know the circumstances in which a child is separated from a parent in order to have any idea what effect it might have for that child.

Some professionals make strong claims about the severe and long-lasting effects any separation has on children. The challenge to those claims made by researchers such as Clarke and Clarke, Rutter and Schaffer offers a much more positive outlook for foster parents, adoptive parents and those who act as a substitute for a child's natural parent.

Personality and attachment

Barbara Tizard (1977) investigated the relationships of adoptive parents with their adopted children who had spent all of their early childhood in residential institutions with little chance to develop stable attachments to an adult.

- Most of the children had become very attached to their adoptive parents.
- Children who had been in residential care and had been returned to their own families did not settle in as well and later showed less-adjusted behaviours than children who had gone to adoptive parents.

Tizard suggested that the adoptive parents had probably tried harder at being parents.

Professor Rudolph Shaffer expressed this well:

> Successful parenting is a matter of particular personality characteristics that need to be identified, not of 'blood'.
>
> (1981, p.13)

It is a matter of how far parents are able to 'dovetail', to be able to adapt to their children's particular needs.

In trying to disentangle the cause and effect of attachment and separation, it is helpful to remember Clarke and Clarke's comment, that a child 'is not a passive receptor of stimulation, but rather is an increasingly dynamic being, who to some extent *causes* his own learning experiences' (1976, p. 13). How children interact with their parents has an effect upon how their parents behave towards them.

Attachment and growth

How children and their parents interact and form attachments not only influences children's emotional and social behaviours – as already described – but also affects the development of children's thinking. Rutter (1981) suggests that:

- emotional and social growth are affected by attachment, and;
- cognitive growth is influenced by how much stimulation parents offer to their children.

Parents stimulate their children by talking with them and generally encouraging them to engage in mental and physical activities that exercise their abilities.

What are the implications of attachment for practice?

What has emerged from this discussion is that parents' sensitive responses to their offspring are fundamental to children's feelings of security and their healthy physical and psychological development. While it is the parents who first have the opportunity of such a relationship, all who work with children can enjoy it too.

> Anyone who works with children should be attentive to the needs that are special to each child and be prepared and able to adapt to them.

Key questions

Use these questions to check back over the material in the chapter and assess your grasp of it, before moving on. Discuss the questions, and responses to them, with colleagues and tutors.

- What is the evidence that children attach to their parents and other adults?
- What behaviours in children suggest that they are attached to a person?
- What behaviours in others promote children's attachment to them?
- Do separations from people to whom they are attached always result in permanent physical or psychological damage to the children?

Relevant S/NVQ Units

The material in this chapter will help with preparation for the following Child Care and Education S/NVQ Units: C2, C4, C5, E1, P2, P5, P8 and P9.

Further reading

Melhuish, E.C. (1993) *A measure of love? An overview of the assessment of attachment*, Association of Child Psychology and Psychiatry Review and Newsletter, Vol. 16, part 6, pp. 269–275. Written primarily for psychologists and psychiatrists, this is a useful appraisal of different ways of trying to measure children's attachments to parents.

Pilling, D. and Pringle, M. Kellmer (1978) *Controversial Issues in Child Development*, London: Paul Elek. Part 1 'The impact of very early life experiences on development'. Not only is this a detailed discussion of attachment but it offers helpful annotations of seminal writings.

Schaffer, R. (1977) *Mothering*, London: Fontana. This book explains in everyday terms the results of the author's researches into relationships between children and their mothers.

Activity

Moving from home to care

The tasks in this activity require you to think about separation and what you could do to reduce the anxieties of children and parents who are about to part at the care agency.

Organization

This activity is broken down into two tasks, which can be completed by individuals or by small groups of not more than five people. Decide which tasks you will complete.

Task 1

1 Write a list of questions which could be used to ask parents about:
   - their thoughts, feelings and actions when they had to leave their children in a crèche, playgroup, or other care facility for the first time, and;
   - how their children reacted. (What were their feelings and actions?)
2 Explaining the purpose of the exercise, ask some parents whether they would like to help you by replying to your questionnaire.
3 Summarize what you discovered in a short, written report or in the form of a talk to other students.

Task 2

1 Discuss ideas for an information pack aimed at reducing children's and parents' anxieties about attending a care facility: childminder, playgroup, day care, family centre, etc. It may be in any format you wish (audio, video, print) and in any style (e.g. strip cartoon).
2 Produce a pilot version.
3 Test it with children, parents and supervisors in your workplace and/or other care provisions for young children.

Activity

Children feeling secure

This activity asks you to examine how sensitive care agencies are to the needs of children who are separating from parents and entering a new situation.

Organization

This activity can be completed by individuals or by small groups of not more than five people.

1 Bearing in mind the effects upon children of separation from a parent, plan an induction programme for children to help them cope with separation and the threats they might perceive of new care-takers in a new environment.
2 Compare your programme with what actually happens in your own and others' care provisions.

2

The emergence of a self-identity

Preview

This chapter describes:

- how the self-concepts that children have about themselves are first shaped by people who are important to them;
- how self-concepts shape attitudes, behaviours and self-esteem;
- ideal self-concepts, a basis for children's conscience and moral thinking;
- the ways in which children behave in order to fit in with the image they have of themselves;
- how we can understand children better if we know about their self-concepts.

Self-concepts

People's views about themselves affect many different aspects of their physical and mental health. Children's opinions about themselves – their self-concepts – also influence every part of their lives. Sometimes, children's achievements at school can be predicted more accurately from their views about themselves than from intelligence tests.

Some would say that just as the heart is the engine for people's physical health, self-concepts are the driving force for their psychological health. If self-concepts have such a powerful influence on our lives, we need to know as much as possible about where they come from and why we have these ideas about ourselves.

Independence from parents

A secure relationship with a parent is very important for the development of a child's emotional security, as was emphasized in Chapter 1. A baby's emotional security grows out of a close physical relationship with mother or father, or their substitutes.

Children gradually become more physically independent of parents. As they grow older, children begin to feel secure enough to be out of sight of their parents: for example, to play in the garden or street with neighbours' children. What sustains this feeling of security? At first, it is because children can retreat quickly to be physically close to their parents. But the time comes when that physical security is not readily available – for example, in day care, community playgroups or nursery schools. How can children feel secure when they are so physically detached from their main carer?

An important part of the answer is that children take a bit of their parents with them. Sometimes it is a concrete reminder, something their mother or father has given them which serves as a symbol of the bond, such as a toy or an article of clothing.

The greatest security which children can take into a new situation, without the support of a parent's physical presence, is a sense of identity which allows them to feel secure about themselves. Research has confirmed repeatedly that a person's sense of self is central to becoming psychologically and physically independent.

A strong sense of self allows people to become autonomous, that is, prepared to rely upon themselves.

How self-concepts grow

If a sense of self is so important, we need to know how it comes about and where it comes from. Ask yourself how you know you are good, all right or poor at child care. You might say that you know you are capable because you understand what you read about child care and that you work well with young children. Then, when you think more about it, you might say that your teachers, placement supervisors and colleagues tell you that you are good.

These are the ways in which we develop our self-concepts:

- We have feelings and thoughts about ourselves and these are confirmed or denied by what others tell us about ourselves.
- Sometimes we change our views because of feedback from others, sometimes we do not.
- If we value the opinion of others because they are significant persons in our lives, then we are more likely to change our self-view in response to their comments about us.

Physical self

If self-concepts are shaped by opinions we have about ourselves and others' evaluations of us, when does all this start? Can a baby have a self-concept?

The view of many psychologists is that a baby's self-concept begins as soon as he or she demonstrates a self-awareness. It seems that infants become aware of their physical selves first.

> The first aspect we encounter is the bodily me. It seems to be composed of streams of sensations that arise within the organism – from viscera, muscles, tendons, joints, vestibular canals, and other regions of the body. The technical name for the bodily sense is coenesthesis. . . The infant, apparently, does not know that such experiences are 'his'. But they surely form a necessary foundation for his emerging sense of self. The baby who first cries from unlocalized discomfort will, in the course of growth, show progressive ability to identify the distress as his own.
>
> (Gordon W. Allport, 1955, pages 41–42)

Whenever a parent moves a baby from close body contact (for example, by putting her or him into a cot after being nursed), the baby is made aware that he or she is a physical being separate from that parent. Otherwise, babies might experience themselves to be merely a physical extension of their mother.

This sense of a physical self grows as babies explore their bodies by touching themselves, by bumping against objects, by experiencing body sensations when being dressed and undressed, and so on.

Shaping by 'significant others'

Before infants begin to understand basic words (their name and words like 'good, 'bad', etc.), they rely upon non-verbal signals from their parents and other carers. Non-verbal information includes the smiles, touches and cuddles of carers.

Infants learn to attend to human faces soon after birth, and to experience the various moods conveyed by adults' different facial expressions. Adults give prolonged, adoring smiles to babies, hoping for a smiling response in return. An infant becomes aware of a carer's mood by signals such as tension in the carer's arms. From these non-verbal signs, infants learn about the attitudes and feelings which 'significant adults' have towards them.

> As infants develop a vocabulary, their views about themselves are affected by what they hear significant people say about them.

As infants begin to understand words and then to use them, they hear things about themselves: 'Good boy', 'Hello Michael'. Oft-repeated words from other people tell the infant that he or she has a 'verbal identity tag' – he is Michael or she is Rebecca. Other words signal the feelings of significant others towards him or her: 'Naughty boy', 'Clever girl'. From this verbal information, an infant begins to develop a sense of identity – of being Michael or Rebecca and of having particular attributes.

Ideal self-concept

Young children adopt as their own the expectations which significant others, particularly parents, have for them. Usually it is during adolescence that a person begins to become less dependent upon parents' beliefs; they become more self-reliant. But young children accept the beliefs expressed by significant adults (parents, the clergy, teachers, etc.) and try to behave in ways consistent with those beliefs.

A child's ideal self-concept is the child's view of what sort of person he or she would most like to be. 'Rules' from others form the basis of young children's ideal self-concepts.

Children strive to meet the standards imposed by significant people because they value their affection and wish to be acceptable to them. If significant people show love towards a child, that child feels good about himself or herself, a worthwhile person. Children wish to behave in ways which gain such approval. They become for them the ideal or best ways of behaving.

> When these ideal behaviours have to do with right and wrong – like not telling lies or not stealing – these moral behaviours become part of a child's conscience.
> Children might feel guilty when they fall short of their ideal moral behaviours.

Self-esteem

Self-esteem is the regard people have for themselves. Children may set themselves unattainable ideals, as a result of the expectations that significant people have of them.

Children regard themselves as failures when they are unable to reach their high self-ideals. Constant experiences of failure can result in children devaluing themselves. When children consider themselves to be falling short of their own expectations and become less accepting of themselves, their self-esteem suffers. They develop a lower estimation of their own worth.

Even before a child can understand spoken words, parents can convey disapproval or disappointment by facial expressions, bodily gestures or tone of voice. From a very early stage in a child's life, parents are establishing expectations which the child might build into his or her ideal self.

Children who perceive themselves as failures have a low self-esteem. As a result, children with a low self-esteem lack confidence in their ability to achieve what they set out to do. These children are more easily persuaded by others, they are less self-reliant. They are more likely to copy other children's behaviours because they don't have a high opinion of their own ability to do the right thing. Have you noticed any 'sheep' among the children in your workplace? Do they usually follow another child's lead rather than their own inclination because of a low self-esteem, or for some other reason?

Adults must have realistic expectations for children so that children can meet them and feel good about themselves.

It is important to encourage a positive self-esteem – a sense of self-worth – in children.

Ego-extension

Young children's sense of identity can be seen in their distress when others are careless about their possessions. Just as a baby might be regarded as a physical extension of a mother, a toy or article of clothing can become a physical extension of a child. A misuse of this possession, such as a child snatching another child's hat and kicking it along the floor, can be experienced as a personal attack. In the same way, parents might experience attacks on their children as attacks on themselves.

Things which children think of as belonging to them are known as ego-extensions. These might include attitudes as well as objects. Children (and some adults) can become aggressive when someone criticises 'their' soccer club or their beliefs. Conflicts between Ulster loyalists and Irish nationalists, between Israelis and Palestinians and between factions in Bosnia reflect explosive mixes of personally held political and religious beliefs.

Anything people think of as their own is important to their sense of identity.

Children's sex identity is an important part of their self-concept. The development of a sex identity is discussed in Chapter 3.

The self-concept jigsaw

Children form self-views or self-concepts about most aspects of themselves. They will have views about their physical appearance and physical skills, their musical talents, their educational achievements in reading or number, and so on. Therefore, although writers refer to a self-concept, it might be more accurate to refer to a person's self-concepts.

To understand a child's self-view, we need to learn as much as we can about their self-concepts. These self-concepts are the individual pieces which link together to form the child's jigsaw. If we can understand the relationship between the individual pieces in the self-concept jigsaw, we will discover much about what influences the child's attitudes and behaviours towards himself or herself and towards others.

As children develop, their ideas about themselves become more complex and they become better able to tell others about how they see themselves. Their ability to reason expands and so does their ability to voice their thoughts. Young children are very 'concrete' in their thinking and their insights into themselves. Their self-descriptions tend to be in terms of their physical attributes, for example: 'I have black hair.' 'I am a boy.' 'I can ride a bike.' As children mature into adolescence, they can be more abstract when describing themselves: 'I am a kind person.' 'I am a humanist.'

In trying to encourage children to reveal their self-concepts, it is necessary to use materials and methods which are appropriate to their stage of development.

Self-consistency

Generally speaking, people tend to behave in ways that are consistent with their self-concepts. A young girl with a positive self-concept about her athletic ability will be prepared to show her prowess at climbing, running or some other physical activity.

Children hold on to particular self-concepts:

- as long as their behaviours and ideas remain consistent with their self-view, and;
- while feedback from significant adults and peers reinforces that self-view.

If the same young girl were to keep falling off the climbing frame and constantly trail behind her peers when running, she would develop a different self-concept about her athletic ability. Feedback from her peers and from adults about her climbing and running abilities might also challenge that self-concept and cause her to modify it.

How enduring or stable a self-concept will prove to be in a person's life depends upon how important it is for the person's self-esteem and self-ideal. Sometimes children realise that the way they are behaving contradicts their self-view, or someone else points this out. For example, a boy might consider himself good at sport because he wishes to be like his father who is a professional soccer player. Therefore, he will tend to ignore for as long as possible his own or others' evidence that he is not good at sport.

A person's self-concepts steer what they believe, think and do throughout each stage of life and across every aspect of their living. Therefore, the concepts young children develop about themselves are important. Carers and educators of young children should make themselves aware of how children regard themselves and encourage them to accept themselves positively.

Key questions

Use these questions to check back over the material covered in this chapter and assess your grasp of it, before moving on. Discuss the questions, and your responses to them, with colleagues and tutors.

- What is a self-concept?
- In what ways do children reveal their self-concepts?
- How are self-concepts formed and modified?
- Why are children's self-concepts important for their psychological health?

Relevant S/NVQ Units

The material in this chapter will help with preparation for the following Child Care and Education S/NVQ Units: C2, C4, C5, C9 and C11.

Further reading

Burns, R.B. (1979) *The Self-concept in Theory, Measurement, Development and Behaviour*, London: Longman. The following sections will offer a fuller account of the development and relevance of self-concepts in children's lives: 'A: The history and theory of the self concept' and 'C: Developmental issues'.

Samuels, Shirley C. (1977) *Enhancing Self-concept in Early Childhood*, New York: Human Sciences Press. Chapter 8 'Social self-concept' gives interesting suggestions to promote attitudes that are non-sexist, accepting of cultural diversity and enhancing of feelings about family.

Activity

Self – a separate identity

This activity encourages ways of promoting children's positive awareness of their physical selves and their sense of being a separate identity from those around them.

Organization

The tasks in this activity are suitable for individual or group completion. Groups should have about five members in them. Allow 20 minutes for 1 and 2 combined.

1. Read the following list of suggestions about ways in which we might help children to be more aware of, accept and own a physical self.
2. Decide which you consider to be the best suggestion and give it a rank of 1. Rank the next best 2, and so on, until you have ranked all 15 suggestions.
3. Add to this list any ideas of your own for promoting children's awareness and acceptance of their physical self. [Allow 10 minutes.]
4. Write down five reasons why such a sense of physical self might be important to children's personal and social life. [Allow 10 minutes.]

Here are some suggestions for ways to help children to be more aware of, accept and own their physical self.

Using photographs of children:
(a) Have a named photograph of each child on a display board.
(b) Use a child's photograph to mark his or her clothes peg.
(c) Use a photograph to identify a special place on a wall for a child to display drawings, paintings, birthday cards, etc.
(d) Have a group of children name each child on a group photograph and say how they recognize that person.
(e) Encourage children to use photographs of themselves at different ages in a 'Life Book' and ask them to compare them.

Labelling self:
(f) Put name tags on children's belongings.
(g) Refer to children by name whenever possible and encourage their peers to do the same.
(h) Incorporate each child's name into a story or song and ask them to indicate when they notice it.
(i) Play 'blind man's bluff' – where a blindfolded child has to name the child they catch and describe how they identified that child.
(j) Divide children into pairs and ask each child to draw the other. Put no identification on the drawings and then ask all the children to guess which child each drawing represents.

Charting physical attributes:
(k) Chart children's heights, hair colour, foot size, etc.
(l) Record each child's voice and see whether the group of children can identify who is speaking.
(m) Video record children's play activities and show them to the children to allow them to see themselves as others see them physically.
(n) Display a birthday record of all the children – each child's photograph could be put beside their name.
(o) Mount a large mirror on a wall and encourage children to look into it ('Look here and you'll see a nice person.') and to describe what they see.

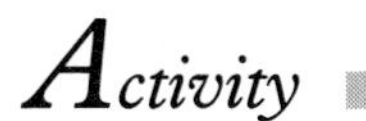

Self-identity: a personal jigsaw

The aim of this activity is to aid children's awareness and acceptance of their physical selves, so that they have a sense of 'owning' their bodies. 'Owning' includes knowing it, liking it, sensing it is personal and belongs to them, protecting it from harm from things and persons outside it, learning to be happy with the body they have – in general, to accept it and take responsibility for it.

Organization

The tasks in this activity are suitable for individual or group completion. Groups should have about five members in them.

Materials needed

- A piece of paper, slightly larger than the full size of each of the children taking part. (Wallpaper is probably the most suitable because it can be obtained cheaply and is thick.)
- A dark-coloured, thick crayon.
- A pair of safety scissors.

Procedure

1 Place the wallpaper, reverse side uppermost, on the floor.
2 Ask a child to lie face up on the paper, with arms, legs and fingers spread enough to allow you to trace around them. (Do not try to persuade cooperation from children who

change their minds about helping in this exercise. Occasionally, children find they dislike it after they have begun.)

3 Draw around the outline of the child.
4 Cut around the outline on the paper, to obtain a cut-out template of the child.
5 Divide the shape into 'jigsaw' pieces by drawing wavy lines, dividing it into five or so large segments. (More segments can always be drawn later, if needed.) Do not cut it into jigsaw pieces, as children might find this threatening.

Development:
There are a variety of ways this template might be used to promote awareness and acceptance of physical self. Here are some suggestions. Try your own ideas too.

1 Consult with the workplace supervisor about selecting a suitable child and whether you need to approach the parent(s) for permission to try the activity.
   - You could say to the child, 'Can you tell me about all the parts that go together to make *you* – nobody else, just you.'
   - Obviously, guide and prompt the child: 'Well, I can think of a piece. What about your hair . . . what colour is it?' Write 'brown hair' (or whatever) on one of the jigsaw pieces on the template.
   - Remember to ensure that one of the jigsaw areas has the child's *name* on it. (That is, unless you plan to use a group of children – see 3 below.)
   - Proceed like this until you have a range of physical descriptions on the jigsaw pieces. Give positive feedback as you enter each item. ('Yes, your hair is a lovely colour, isn't it?' etc.) Discourage non-physical descriptions because these will be incorporated into the jigsaw on later occasions, when gender identity and self-esteem are dealt with.
   - Put the resulting template on the wall, again with appropriate, positive feedback: for example, 'Now you can see just how nice you look, can't you?'

2 Instead of asking a child for a self-description you could invite children in the group to offer them. This needs skilful handling, so that positive descriptions are given. Usually, rewarding the types of description you want achieves this: 'Yes, that's a good one. What other nice things have you noticed about (name of child)?'
3 If templates are made for a group of children, their names could be left off and children invited to guess to whom they belong. This encourages children as a group to notice each other as *individuals* and helps each child to feel that they are individually acknowledged.
4 Remember to salvage the template for any workshop or course file you are keeping! Explain to the owner that you would like to show him or her to your friends . . . or for whatever purpose you wish to borrow or use the child's template.

3

Children's gender awareness

Preview

Present-day society is concerned about treating people differently because they are different sexes. Where does our sexual identity and gender awareness come from? This chapter considers:

- how children develop a gender identity;
- children's learning of a gender role;
- how gender identity and role affect children's attitudes and influence the games they play and the friends they make.

Becoming female or male

Various terms are used to discuss the development of children's awareness of gender. Most writers on this subject distinguish between:

- a child's biological sex type (physiologically, a child is either a male or a female);
- gender identity (a child's feelings of being a boy or a girl, believing his or her characteristics are those of a male or a female);
- gender-role identity (the behaviours which children display to show which gender they feel themselves to be).

Children learn a gender role from adults and other children because those people are important to them and they want to be accepted by them. So, children try to do what those 'significant people' expect of them, listening to what others tell them about gender, what it means to be masculine or feminine. In this way, children develop a concept of the characteristics of a male or female gender role.

Society teaches children what is appropriate to their sex. This includes:

- the physical attributes that are expected of boys compared with girls;
- feelings that are expected of girls but not of boys and vice versa;
- ways of behaving that are distinctively masculine and others that are distinctively feminine.

Studies of children's thinking reveal that young children make sense of their world more through what they see than through ideas.

A young friend came running in one day to tell me that the house was moving. What he had seen was the clouds moving over the rooftop towards him, giving the illusion that the house was moving away from him. An older child would not necessarily have believed what she saw, if it had conflicted with what she knew; she would have reasoned it out. In the same way, younger children make greater use of what they see when sorting females from males: clothes, body shapes, hair, games played, and so on.

Gender-role behaviours

Children learn from society to expect boys to be verbally and physically more aggressive than girls. Girls are viewed by children as more nurturant (concerned for the welfare of others); they are regarded as more kindly, caring and sensitive. 'Doll talk' among children under five years of age indicates their different perceptions of girls' behaviours compared with boys' behaviours. Children usually consider fathers to be more dangerous and more punitive than mothers. How many mothers might use the threat, 'Wait until your father comes home!'?

Stories for children confirm these stereotypes. (A gender stereotype is a pattern of behaviour which society thinks is appropriate for either males or females.) Boys' games interests are expected to show a bias towards those which display physical prowess and activity, while girls are expected to be more interested in less active pursuits – in clothes and dolls, for instance.

Some researchers disagree that children's gender-role behaviours are learned. They think that gender-role behaviours originate from inborn biological differences between males and females. Reviewing a variety of researches, Archer (1992) reports that differences between the sexes in play and activity can be seen in children as young as 13 months and that this difference is consistent across various age-groups of young children. He concludes that early differences in play probably originate not from any learning of stereotypes of gender preferences for toys but because of different activity levels and interaction styles for boys and girls based on biological differences between them.

Children from 33 months to 60 months of age have been found to play more actively in same-sex groupings. But in mixed sex groups, boys were invariably more active than girls and, in competitive situations, dominated girls. Research has also shown that lower-social-class mothers reinforce gender typing more than middle-class mothers. Lower-class children from three to eight years of age show gender attitudes and behaviours which are close to the stereotypes.

People's beliefs about covert attributes (people's hidden qualities) in males and females are also biased.

- Females are considered to have an *expressive* role, experiencing feelings about people.
- Males are considered to have an *instrumental* role, focusing upon doing things.

> Children come to think of themselves as either boys or girls as a result of what they see and hear about the sexes during their development. This is called their gender identity.

Gender-role identity

From soon after birth, our experiences of people and events around us start to shape our sex-role identity. Through our gender-role behaviours, we indicate to others whether we feel ourselves to be a male or a female.

As infants, we begin to associate some attributes, behaviours and clothes with mothers and others with fathers. Brothers and sisters, more often than not, make the same distinctions. Verbal and non-verbal feedback from these significant people in young children's lives encourage behaviours which society considers to be appropriate for their gender. Family members reward boys for being a 'chip off the old block' and girls for copying mothers' behaviours round the house. In this way, infants begin to identify quite strongly with the parent of the same sex and learn to copy appropriate gender-typed behaviours.

As they become older, children watch and copy the gender-role behaviours of mates and adults whom they admire, outside of their immediate family. They copy the gender-role behaviours of same-sex children and adults they meet in the neighbourhood, at school and in other groups they belong to (such as sports clubs and leisure centres, organizations such as cubs and scouts, brownies and guides). Increasingly, it is being realized just how much children model their gender-role behaviours on people they see on television.

> The combined influence of parents, family, school and media, are powerful determinants of a child's gender-role identity.

Problems might occur for children when the gender-type behaviours they have acquired from one of these influences fail to match those considered appropriate by one of the groups they belong to or by society at large. For example, a father might show behaviours and sensitivities towards his children which are regarded by the social group among whom he lives as more appropriate to women. A son who models himself on such a father might display similar behaviours at the neighbourhood school and could be rejected by his peers.

> By three years of age, most children can describe themselves accurately as a boy or a girl.
>
> Around the same age, children have begun to link particular toys, games, clothing, occupations and domestic objects with either boys and men or girls and women.
>
> Although gender identity is bi-polar (male is opposite to female), gender behaviours and interests are not.

Understanding gender identity

The behaviours and interests of people cannot always be separated into those which belong only to men and others which are exclusively associated with women. Young children do not regard helpful, sympathetic and aggressive behaviours to be characteristics only of men or women; but some pre-school children believe that boys are noisy and girls are quiet and nice.

At around seven years of age children begin to understand that sex identity is constant. As children develop, they begin to realize that gender identity usually does not change – that a boy is a male and a girl is a female irrespective of what they wear, how they speak, whether their hair is long or short and despite what they might look like.

As they get older, children become better able to distinguish gender attributes which give a clear indication of a person's sex from those which do not. For example, some parts of the body are a reliable indicator of the owner's sex, as are gender clues such as some high-heeled shoes or skirts. But a person's hair length cannot be relied upon absolutely to tell us whether the wearer is male or female.

The gender-links of behaviours are confirmed continually for children by adults and peers around them: for instance, a mother attending to the cooking and washing while a father repairs the car and digs the garden. Younger boys are taught in schools mostly by women, while older boys are taught mostly by men. Education itself teaches occupational gender stereotypes. Women teachers give younger children needed nurturance (welfare), men do not. How many male teachers of infants are there? Are there qualities of human caring which only women can provide for young children?

Messages from the media

> Television, films and children's books reinforce stereotypes.

Children, on average, spend more time watching television than they spend in any other single activity, with the exception of sleep. Perhaps, for some, even sleeping hours are outnumbered by television watching. Huston (1983) reports that analyses of television programmes revealed that males and females are presented in sex-stereotyped roles and that in prime-time screening, two thirds to three quarters of the major characters are males. Females were in the minority in all types of programmes, although in soap operas and comedies the balance was more equal.

The contents of books for children of various ages reveal a similar pattern to that for television. They include more male characters; males tend to be active while females are passive followers and onlookers. Many traditional children's stories reinforce stereotypes for the roles of men and women in the home and in jobs. However, it should be noted that this trend is being reversed in many modern-day stories and publications.

Such high profiling of one sex more than the other can suggest that one sex has a higher status, more value and, therefore, more power. Society sometimes gives a higher status to men. Only in recent years has such unequal valuing of women been checked – with the establishment of equal opportunities, the monitoring of fair employment and a more equal allocation among the sexes of senior positions in industry, commerce and the professions.

Children's gender roles might be influenced by these sorts of inequality that have been a part of our society for many years. Boys tend to be concerned to behave in ways which they believe to be masculine more than girls wish to keep within the bounds of behaviours regarded as feminine.

> The tendency to keep to gender stereotypes becomes more rigid with increasing age.

For boys, behaving like a girl has been found, in Western cultures, to result in a loss of status among their peers, but the converse is not true: behaving like a boy would seem to give greater status to a girl. This applies throughout childhood and into adulthood.

Putting boundaries round gender groups begins with primary school, when children exclude the other sex from their groups. These boundaries remain into adulthood and usually involves some 'put down' of females by males. Boys usually chase girls in kissing games, and adolescent boys often monopolize resources in sciences and computing and denigrate girls' attainments. The sexual harassment of women in the workplace appears to be an extension of the behaviours observable at school age.

Promoting gender awareness in children

Whatever the origin of gender behaviours, adults working with children need to be aware that many of the discriminatory attitudes and behaviours they recognize readily among adults are evident in young children. Children's gender beliefs can affect the outcome of their experiences in playgroup, school or other groups and influence the progress of counselling or psychological therapy, especially family therapy. For example, conflict in a family may originate in a man's chauvinist attitudes and behaviours towards his partner. Changing the family dynamics will be less easy if the children in the family have accepted the gender stereotypes of their father in the home and they express the same attitudes and behaviours as he does towards their mother .

Children bring with them to child-care situations the gender beliefs shaped by significant people in their family, neighbourhood, school and other organizations. Their beliefs about gender can be reinforced or modified as a result of experiences gained in playgroups, family centres and other provisions for the care and education of children.

Many adults are becoming increasingly aware that some of the gender-discriminatory practices in society are not acceptable. But this change has hardly begun among adults who work with younger children. This is all the more poignant when it is pointed out that the majority of workers with young children are women.

The issue of children's gender awareness has wider, political implications. If discrimination against women is an integral part of Britain's history, then part of the task ahead might be to give greater status to early years' workers. While such work continues to be regarded by the male majority which controls the financing of industry and commerce as 'merely' an extension of a nurturant, mothering role it will only be given low status and low priority in the allocation of resources.

Women working with young children need to believe in their own status in order to be effective in the task of creating an awareness of gender and the development of more flexible gender boundaries in those children. Men working in child care and education have a responsibility to support that move, if they are not to be hypocritical in any attempts to promote gender awareness and fairness in children.

Key questions

Use these questions to check back over the material covered in the chapter and assess your grasp of it, before moving on. Discuss the questions, and your responses to them, with colleagues and tutors.

- How do young children come to have beliefs about behaviours which they consider to be appropriate to each sex and gender?
- What attitudes do children you know or work with have towards the play and behaviours of age mates of the opposite sex?
- What might adults do to discourage sexism in children?

Relevant S/NVQ Units

The material in this chapter will help with preparation for the following Child Care and Education Units: C2, C4, C5, C8, C9, C10 and C11.

Further reading

Dunn, Judy (1984) *Sisters and Brothers*, London: Fontana. 'Sex differences', pp. 68–71, 'Same-sex and different-sex children', pp. 83–85, 'Patterns over time: boys and girls', pp. 90–92.

Golombok, S. and Rust, J. (1993) *The measurement of gender-role behaviour in pre-school children: A research note*, in Journal of Child Psychology and Psychiatry, Vol. 34 (5), 805–811. Susan Golombok and John Rust have devised a pre-school activities inventory to assess gender-role behaviour in young children.

Huston, Aletha C. (1983) 'Sex-typing' in Hetherington, E.M. (ed.) and Mussen, P.H. (series ed.), *Handbook of Child Psychology, Volume 4, Socialization, personality and social development*, pp. 387–467, New York: Wiley. This is an academic account for those wishing to pursue the topic in more scientific detail.

Parker, Tony (1969) *The Twisting Lane: Some Sex Offenders*, London: Panther Books. This book gives accounts by sex offenders of their own understanding of their behaviours. It gives glimpses into their histories, which offer insights into what can happen when sex and gender attitudes and behaviours go awry during the developmental span.

Samuels, Shirley C. (1977) *Enhancing Self-concept in Early Childhood*, New York: Human Sciences Press. Chapter 4 'Sex-role identification', pp. 119–145.

Activity

Discouraging sexism in young children

The tasks in this activity encourage ways of counteracting sexism in children.

Organization

This activity is suitable for completion by individuals or groups with five or fewer members.

Task 1

1 Think of well-known stories and nursery rhymes in which the female is weak and is dependent upon the strong, independent male. (The stories should be those you would tend to include in storytimes in your children's

group, but other stories appropriate to young children may be included.) For example, the sleeping beauty is dependent upon the kiss from the prince. Jack of beanstalk fame had a widowed mother who had to rely on her young son to look after her. Make a list.
2 Devise a plot for a story in which there is an inter-dependency between the female and male heroine and hero, where sex identity and gender behaviours have equal status. Alternatively, re-write one of the stories listed in answer to question 1 along these lines.

Task 2
Draw up a list of behaviours you have observed in young children which are clearly stereotypes of males or females.

Task 3
1 Write down what policies you have in your workplace to combat sexism among staff and in children's behaviours and attitudes.
2 In what ways could you improve upon these policies or make them more effective?

Task 4
1 Divide a sheet of paper into three columns.
2 Give the heading 'male' to the first column, 'female' to the next and 'both' to the last column.
3 In the appropriate column enter the toys, materials, equipment and books etc. which you think would be used mainly by boys, girls or both.
4 Compare the items in each column.
   - Which column has the most?
   - Are the items in the boys' or girls' columns ones you would describe as stereotypically male or female?
   - Are there any items you could add to the 'both' column, which your workplace does not have?
   - What have you learned from this activity?

Activity

Exploring gender with children
The aim of the tasks in this activity is to develop skills in talking to children in order to uncover their beliefs about gender.

Organization
This activity is suitable for completion by individuals or groups with five or fewer members.

Task 1
Build on the jigsaw person you completed for the second Activity in Chapter 2. Enter pieces into the 'puzzle of this person' which reflect the child's gender identity. For example, you could use a piece of the jigsaw to reflect the games he or she likes to play, the clothes the child likes wearing best, jobs she or he would like to do when an adult, etc.

Task 2
To explore children's ideas and attitudes about the attributes of females and males, create a set of comic-strip stories which have either a hero or heroine (or both) but leave the story incomplete. You can achieve this by leaving out the last picture completely, and saying to the child, 'The story needs finishing. What will the last picture show? Can you tell me how the story will finish?'

Alternatively, the last picture might allow for a verbal completion of the story by having the characters' speech bubbles blank and, again, prompt the child to complete it: 'Oh look! We can't read what they are saying. What do you think they are saying?' This should give you some indication of how boys and girls might adhere to a stereotype in attributing aggressive qualities, etc. to male characters and dependent qualities, etc. to female characters.

Task 3

Another way of exploring young children's gender preconceptions is to create cut-outs (catalogues and magazines might provide a source) of people in occupational work. If possible, obtain illustrations that allow for the removal of the head and leave a body that is not too clearly one gender or the other. Using a range of these cut-outs, draw or obtain from a magazine a picture of a man's head and a woman's head. Show children each occupational cut-out separately and ask them to put on the head which belongs with each body. This allows children to reveal gender-specific preconceptions about occupations. (If you are able, produce drawings instead of cut-outs to ensure good fits between the parts.)

Task 4

Using a tape recorder, hold interviews with young children, one at a time, to ask, 'What are girls like?' and 'What are boys like?' Both questions should be asked of a number of boys and girls because a measure of stereotypic attitudes should discover what boys think of their own gender and what they think of girls, and vice versa.

Listen to the tapes and compile four lists of comments:

(a) boys about boys;
(b) boys about girls;
(c) girls about girls;
(d) girls about boys.

4

Children's socialization

Preview

This chapter discusses:

- adults' influences upon children's socialization;
- differences between children's interactions with adults and peers;
- empowering children with experiences of appropriate control;
- authoritative compared with authoritarian parenting;
- effective structuring of children's social cognitive efforts;
- children's relationships and friendships;
- ways of promoting children's social competence.

Social beginnings

Children's socialization – the process by which society shapes their beliefs and behaviours – begins with the relationship between baby and mother. From birth, there is a social interaction between child and parent. Changes resulting from the processes of mental and physical growth influence children's relationships with their mothers, which together shape children's development.

A child's development is the outcome of the mental and physical resources he or she brings to the world from the moment of birth and how those resources are used in learning to adapt to the world by interacting with other people. The child's social development is founded on the sensitive responsiveness of parents and then adults in general. Sensitive responsiveness means:

> adults' awareness of children as individual in their own right. It is a continuum. At one end are the optimally sensitive adults who are able to see things from the child's point of view, are alert to the child's signals and communications, can interpret these correctly, and then respond promptly and appropriately. At the other end, are the adults who cannot see the child at all as a separate individual, who distort the child's communications in the light of their own needs, and who interact with the child on the basis of their own wishes rather than the child's.
>
> (Shaffer, 1989, p. 207)

Infants only a few months old pay close attention to features on human faces and to noises that sound like human speech. Because their babies respond, parents bring their faces close to their baby's face and talk to them, even though the baby doesn't comprehend. The pause–suck time sequence to babies' suckling encourages mothers to touch and talk to the baby in the pauses.

Mothers spend comparatively long periods gazing at their babies and respond when the babies look at them. When infants gurgle and babble, parents often have a pretend conversation with them, the parent talking when the baby stops vocalizing. These sorts of turn-taking give the infant an example of how to interact socially, even though that is not the parent's intention.

From birth, babies' interests and behaviours encourage attention from their mothers. From about 20 weeks, the development of infant motor skills (becoming able to control head, hand, arm and leg movements) means that babies become interested in other things besides parental faces. When they are able to grasp hold of things, they become interested in looking at them and taking hold of them. When a baby looks towards some object or toy, a parent more often than not will pay attention to it also, perhaps handing it to the infant and having a pretend conversation about it with the baby. This change in the focus of their interaction – when a parent and child share an active interest in an object – is a crucial one for the child's development.

From around nine months, a baby can begin to follow a pointing finger. It is some time after 12 months that an infant uses pointing to draw an adult's attention to something. Increasingly, parents will give labels to things an infant points at. As children's speech begins to develop, they start to use words to draw their parent's attention to things in which they are interested.

As an infant grows and matures, he or she begins a social interaction process with a parent by looking at, taking hold of, or in some way indicating an interest in something nearby.

With maturation, an infant becomes able to attend to more than one thing at a time. At around 32 weeks, infants begin to shift from dealing with one thing at a time (looking at mother or attending to a toy) to being able to combine activities ('talking' with mother while passing a toy to and fro between them). This type of social interaction is much more reciprocal – that is, mother and child are responding to each other's requests.

Social competence and control

Accounts of children's social development used to emphasize how individual children's maturation (the biological factors guiding growth) influenced their socialization. Researchers such as Rudolph Shaffer, Professor of Psychology at the University of Strathclyde, have shown the importance of also taking a closer look at what is happening in interactions between adults and children. Relationships between parents and children affect many important aspects of children's development. Development means the changes in behaviours, abilities and attitudes as people grow.

The hallmark of successful socialization is a child's ability to guide his or her own behaviours, without constant adult direction. In order to live without adult direction, children need to have some ideas about what to do or say in a range of situations. How strongly children believe in their ideas will determine how long those ideas will guide their behaviours. For example, a girl might be well-mannered because she is more likely to get what she wants if she behaves herself. On another occasion, because she identifies with a close friend, she might adopt that friend's views and behaviours and express them in social groups. But when the friendship ends, she no longer holds on to those views or behaviours. These types of change in behaviour do not last long. If the same girl believed she should treat others in the same way as she wished to be treated, then that belief is more likely to influence her behaviours whatever the circumstances.

> When a child believes in something, it affects behaviour for a longer time and is less easily changed than a view which is held merely to identify or mix socially with others.

Attitudes that are internalized (become part of a child's belief system) can influence the values that make up a child's identity and ego ideal (see Chapter 2). These determine how much other social factors influence the child. For example, if a boy has learned colour and religious prejudice because he is black and a Protestant, then he is more likely to reject any social influences that he sees as white or Catholic.

When children have internalized attitudes, their own beliefs direct their social behaviours from within them, rather than being externally constrained by parental or other people's controls. Shaffer (1989) considers that this happens during the first two years of life. Social development progresses from being primarily other-controlled towards becoming self-controlled. This process is also important for children's moral thinking (see Chapter 7).

What is it about child–parent relationships that results in children's internalization of attitudes? There is no definite answer. Eleanor Maccoby *et al.* (1983) looked thoroughly into this. A number of different research studies with a range of young children up to six years of age show that when parents and adults use powerful, assertive ways of getting children to do things, then the children's obedience is short-lived.

The most effective social pressure which is likely to result in internalization is when parents and adults use enough, but not too much, pressure to persuade a child to comply with their suggestions. This method is likely to be effective because a child can still attribute any change to himself or herself, thus retaining a feeling of some control over what is happening. The feeling that what happens is within their own power (having an 'internal locus of control') enhances children's self-esteem and helps to offset the health threats of life's stresses. (People who have a sense of control in their lives and in their jobs are less prone to illness resulting from stress.) Parents who are sensitive, attuned to their children's needs, responsive to children's abilities by adapting their own responses to them – foster this sense of personal competence and control.

Children form secure attachments to parents who are accepting, cooperative, sensitive, show emotional warmth towards them, and who are sociable and available whenever needed. Children who are securely attached show 'receptive' compliance – a willingness to cooperate with their parents.

> Children are more likely to show socially self-controlled behaviour when parents encourage them to be independent, to rely upon themselves.

When parents explain, reason and appeal to children's sympathy for others and desire to be more grown up, children become more competent socially. Therefore, to help children's social development, adults need to encourage their sense of control over events. Being either too domineering or too unassertive with children can remove their feeling of being able to influence what happens around them.

Authoritative not authoritarian parenting

Baumrind (1971) studied different types of parental behaviours and their influence upon the children at pre-school and, in a follow-up observation, during their middle primary years. Authoritarian parents do not encourage their children to discuss matters with them; they want their children to be obedient and to respect authority unquestioningly. They try to control their children and tend to judge them according to a rigid set of standards. Not only do they demand much, they are also not very responsive towards their children.

Authoritative parents have a clear set of standards but recognize their own and their children's rights and are prepared to listen to their children's points of view. They encourage a child to be an individual and to be independent, expecting competence and maturity from their children. However, they are prepared to enforce rules and standards appropriately. These parents tend to be demanding of their children but at the same time are highly responsive to their needs.

Pre-school children of authoritative parents were found to be socially more competent and independent than the children of authoritarian parents. Socially competent 8–9 year olds have parents who make high demands but who listen to their children and respond appropriately.

> A parent or adult needs to be authoritative but not authoritarian.

Social interaction and development

Shaffer (1992) pointed to the importance of interactions between parents and young children. This consists of a parent and a child working on something together; for example, building a construction toy. Shaffer refers to such sessions as Joint Involvement Episodes (JIEs). A JIE could also consist of two children working together. At present, there is an interest in whether JIEs between mothers (or another adult) and children or between two children are more effective in influencing children's learning and development.

> Interactions between mothers and their infants affect most aspects of children's development, not only social development but also developments in children's thinking and language.

Which contributes more to children's socialization: their interactions with their parents or with their peers? The evidence so far suggests that a dyad (a group of two) consisting of a very young child and a parent or adult helps a child's development more than a dyad of two very young children. But children at school have been found to be better at problem-solving when in pairs than when working alone, irrespective of whether they had a less able or more able partner.

A simple explanation is that a very young child cannot give the required help that an adult can. With increasing age, children are able to give this help to someone their own age. There is a growing interest in the extent to which groups larger than pairs might influence children's development.

Focusing children's attention

A parent's contribution was called 'scaffolding' by Jerome Bruner (1975). This describes the types of parental support mentioned earlier, especially when parents adapt to a child's progress with a task. Pre-school children's attention and concentration increase when adults join in their activities.

Adults help children to structure their attention, focusing them upon the different aspects of a situation. This is a crucial help.

> Parents give a structure or scaffold to support children's efforts.
> Adults who most effectively support children's efforts keep one step ahead of the children's progress and draw their attention to the next relevant part of the task.

The importance of this is that it feeds the child with alternatives to what he or she is thinking at that moment, and challenges the child to respond by retaining or changing ideas. Shaffer thinks that this could explain why young children are not as effective as adults are at being social partners for other young children. Older children are better able to present alternative ideas, to create a contrasting view which can promote progress in the thinking of a partner of their own age or younger.

Effective interaction

When adults join children in their play activities:

- children attend and concentrate on a task for longer periods of time;
- they think and reason more.

Research indicates that adults who work together with children on a problem, rather than merely observing and giving advice, make a greater contribution to the children's thinking and to their later ability to cope with the task alone.

Where care or education provisions for young children have too few adult staff, the value of encouraging and training parents and other adult helpers should be considered. Two or three members of staff caretaking large groups of children who are left free for most of the time to wander in unstructured play activities may betray the children's potential and may fail to harness their zest for living.

> It is important for professional carers and educators to interact on a one-to-one basis with children as much as possible.
> It is evident that interaction in dyads between children and parents or other adults contributes significantly to the development of children's thinking.

Children's relationships

An emphasis upon parent–child interactions can cause us to neglect children's relationships. Interactions are particular behaviours that we can see and measure. We make assumptions about relationships from watching interactions. For instance, we assume an attachment relationship when we see the interactions of sensitive, communicative and nurturant behaviours from a mother towards an infant and how the infant runs towards the mother and is distressed at her absence. We can describe and watch the mother's and infant's behaviours (their interactions), but we tend to describe the relationship by using examples of interactions.

Children are involved in different sorts of relationship:

- relationships can be very close and enduring, such as loving relationships between members of a family or the closeness of friendships;
- other relationships are not close like this, for example acquaintances such as with other young children at playgroup or pupils in a class.

Children do not have relationships with strangers, yet they have different types of interactions with them, responding positively to some and negatively to others. Studies have not yet investigated the richness of all these types of relationships for children; they have focused primarily upon attachment relationships. The importance of any particular relationship for a child cannot be understood without seeing it in the context of the total pattern of relationships in that child's life.

> The role of mothers in children's relationships is given more attention than that of fathers, siblings, other relatives, significant adults or peers.
>
> In trying to understand a particular child, professionals should not make decisions on the basis of any single relationship, without taking into account other relationships that might be important.

Children's friendships

To understand children's social development, we need to know about their relationships with other children, especially peers. As might be expected, relationships with friends are different from those with parents or other adults. Children can interact with each other as equals.

William Hartup, Professor of Child Psychology at the University of Minnesota, is an authority on children's peer relationships. He concludes that while children's peer friendships are not necessary to the process of development, they evidently bring advantages to it. In a recent review of the significance of children's friendships for their development, he discusses the interesting findings of a number of researchers (Hartup, 1992).

> Younger children have fewer friends than older children and adolescents who, on average, mention about five times more best friends.
>
> Younger friendships do not last as long as those of older children and adolescents.

Most friendships begin as a result of children being involved in something together, enjoying common interests. With young children the activity of doing things together is a foundation to the friendship: I lend him my toys and he lends me his. Older children are more aware of the personal aspects to the relationship: sympathy, loyalty, shared confidences, etc.

Younger children's social interactions take the form of play; older children's have more to do with personal and social relationships. Children's friendships with peers allow them to learn, on an equal footing, the trials and tribulations of relationships with non-family members. In friendships, children learn to be cooperative, to return their partner's kindnesses, to handle disagreements and they learn concern for others. These well-learnt lessons help children to become more capable in other social situations. Hartup mentions an investigation of 4154 pre-school dyads by Howes (1989) which shows that stable friendships encourage greater social competence. That competence lessens when the friendship stops.

The exercising of existing social skills and the learning of new ones in such friendships means that children are more likely to be successful in developing friendships within other relationships. Friendships between children can offer security for them in new or strange situations, such as a playgroup or school. They can share problem tasks, confidences, feelings and so on which helps their adjustment to those circumstances.

In care and education provision, it is good practice to promote the formation of friendships among children and to watch for children who do not appear to have a friend. This could support children who are settling into new surroundings and help them to cope with each day's new social demands.

Promoting children's social competence

Summarizing this account of children's socialization, the following pointers should guide professional carers' and educators' practice in seeking to support children's social development:

1 Workers should enable parents to develop a positive approach to sharing tasks with their children.
2 In day nurseries, crèches, playgroups and nursery schools in particular, workers should spend time in appropriate, one-to-one interaction with children.
3 Management of children should avoid the extremes of either being domineering or too unassertive. Through a sensitive awareness of the children, staff should discover what level of persuasion is best for each child in their care.
4 Workers should encourage children to be independent by asking their views about decisions and changes which might affect them.
5 Clear, but not inflexible, standards for behaviour should encourage children to make up their own minds and, within a secure social framework, to learn how to have an effect upon events they are involved in.
6 Children should feel that the significant adults in their lives regard them as worthwhile people and respect them as individuals. Staff working with children should be prepared to adapt to their needs and acknowledge their rights.

Key questions

Use these questions to check back over the material covered in the chapter and assess your grasp of it, before moving on. Discuss the questions, and responses to them, with colleagues and tutors.

- What are the early signs of social activity between parents and their children?
- How do shared activities between adults and children help children's development?
- Do authoritarian or authoritative parents contribute more to children's social learning?
- Why do child-care workers need to be watchful of children's friendships?

Relevant S/NVQ Units

The material in this chapter will help with preparation for the following Child Care and Education S/NVQ Units: C2, C4, C5, C7, C9, C10, C11, C14, E1, M8 and P2.

Further reading

Bremner, J.G. (1988) *Infancy*, Oxford: Basil Blackwell. Chapter 5, pp. 152–171, usefully expands upon what is covered in this chapter regarding infants' perceptions of faces and voices and gives a general background to infant emotions; pp. 191–210 add to the discussion of how parents' social communications contribute to children's language development.

Rubin, Z. (1980) *Children's Friendships*, London: Fontana. A very readable book with a wealth of information about children's friendships and how to be sensitive to them.

Shaffer, H.R. (1992) 'Joint Involvement Episodes as context for development' in McGurk, H. (ed.) *Childhood Social Development: Contemporary Perspectives*, Hove, UK: Lawrence Erlbaum Associates. Chapter 4, pp. 99–129, gives details of how adults help children's cognitive development in one-to-one interactions.

Activity

Children, friendship and emotions

The aim of this activity is to prepare individuals to compare two dyads (remember a dyad is a group of two people):

- dyad 1 = a parent and young child;
- dyad 2 = two young children.

If possible, plan to study children younger than two years of age.

Preparation

Check through chapter 4 for differences between the ways an adult interacts with a child and the ways two children interact.

Organization

For individual or group activity.

1 Design a chart along the following lines on an A4 page.
   - Down the left-hand side, put a list of behaviours which you expect to see between mother and child in dyad 1 and between the two children in dyad 2.

- Divide the width of the page into columns, allowing one column for every five minutes of time you will spend observing at each meeting. (For example, if your observation sessions are 30 minutes, you should allow six columns.)
- You will need one of these charts for each observation session.

2 Plan how the study will be conducted. This should include these considerations:
- How many meetings with each dyad are desirable and how long should each meeting be?
- What words will be used and what procedures will be followed for the adult–child dyad and for the child–child one?
- How will you arrange for each member of the group to conduct the study? This should be organized in consultation with your tutor.

3 Complete a detailed account of your observations. Record the behaviours you see by:
- writing at the top of the page the name of the dyad you are observing and the date and time of the observation;
- putting a tick in one of the columns beside each behaviour to show in which five minutes of the observation period you saw it.

4 If you are part of a group, arrange a meeting to discuss the findings of each member. Individuals should list differences they noticed between the two pairs.

Activity

Talking to children about their friends

This activity has three aims:
- to engage you in a conversation with a child, and thereby;
- to listen carefully to the child, and;
- to analyse what you learn about the child's friendships.

Preparation
Read 'Children's friendships' in Chapter 4 (see p.32), highlighting which aspects of relationships it is important to know about in order to understand the characteristics of friendships at particular ages.

Organization
This activity may be completed by individuals or small groups of about five members.

1 Decide whether you wish to study a single-age group of children or to compare one age group with another.
2 Individuals: spend a few minutes writing questions which could be asked of a child to discover as much as possible about his or her peer friendships.
3 For groups: the group leader should read out his or her list and each group member who has a different question to suggest should read it out.
4 As a group or as an individual, decide which questions will be included in the final list. (Remember to avoid a lengthy list and repeating questions. Keep your questions simple. They should not intrude into a child's personal or family life. Check with your tutor or with a senior person caring for the children that your questions are acceptable.)
5 Individuals should use these questions to interview children about their friendships, making a written record of their replies.
6 Groups should arrange a meeting to discuss their findings, comparing replies from different age groups, if two or more have been interviewed. Individuals should compare their findings with what we and others say about children's friendships.

5

Understanding and alleviating children's anxieties

Preview

This chapter examines:

- children's everyday anxieties;
- physical and psychological signs of anxiety in children;
- distinctions between children's fears, phobias and panics;
- the fears from which children's anxieties may arise;
- what might be done to lessen children's fears and anxieties;
- when to seek more specialist help.

Common fears and anxieties

Anxiety is related to a fear of something.
Some children's fears are related to their age.

At some time or another all children display anxiety. Children have fears about people, places, things or thoughts in their real, imagined or dream worlds which make them anxious. Children of similar ages fear similar things. Some fears are characteristic of young children, some of older children and others are found across all age groups. When surveying more than 6000 children in Buckinghamshire aged between 5 and 15, Shepherd, Oppenheim and Mitchell (1971) found that about half of the five-year-olds were anxious about animals and the dark. The proportion of children showing these particular fears lessened among the older ones.

A recent comparison of the ten greatest fears reported by boys and girls between 8 and 10 years in Britain found that they were almost identical to those reported by American and Australian children (Ollendick, Yule and Ollier, 1991). This suggests that, whatever the culture, children's fears are very similar.

In the Buckinghamshire study, at all ages, more girls than boys were reported to show some degree of fear towards some animals. Up to nine years of age, twice as many girls as boys showed this fear. In the comparison of American, Australian and British children, girls were found to have a greater fear than boys of the unknown, of minor injury, of animals and of danger and death. Clearly, girls and boys differ in their fears.

Differences in fears between boys and girls might have something to do with the sex-role standard of a society, boys being less prepared than girls to admit to some fears.

When asking ourselves whether a particular child's fears are similar to those of most other children, we need to take into consideration the age and sex of the child. It is not fully understood why fears and anxieties change with age and gender. One suggestion is that it is linked with the development of children's thinking ability and self-esteem. If a child does not fully understand something, it means that he or she feels less control over it.

> It might be threatening not to understand something and not to be able to control it. Threats arouse anxieties.

Different research has produced different lists of fears for different ages of children (see the suggestions for further reading at the end of this chapter). Rather than learn lists of fears for different ages, it might be more useful to recognize when children are anxious and then to discover what is frightening them.

> Children give physical and psychological signals of their anxieties.

Physical and psychological signals of anxiety

Physical signals of anxiety

1. Children give us physical signals such as trembling, shaking or crying and movement.
2. They will resist coming into contact with whatever it is they fear – not touching particular things, avoiding being with a person who frightens them, refusing to visit or to look at them, not running to greet them, running away or not entering places that frighten them. Young children might cling to parents and become violent should anyone try to separate them.
3. Anxiety can cause wetting or soiling, a flushed or pale face, damp palms and foreheads, breathing difficulties and vomiting in some cases.

Psychological signals of anxiety

1. Children might tell friends or adults their feelings and thoughts about something they fear. Sometimes, if they feel awkward about mentioning their fears, they will reveal them in a roundabout or disguised way. Adults who work with children must listen to what children say.
2. A child might be preoccupied, appear to be daydreaming, be irritable and unable to concentrate when their fear becomes too much for them.
3. Children dream about their fears, sometimes in the form of nightmares.
4. Creative activities often provide a medium through which children might express frightening thoughts: paintings, stories, puppet or roleplay activities, sand or water play.

Some anxieties are about things external to a child. For example, children may fear dogs, strange people and places. Ideas generated mainly by a child's own thoughts can cause anxiety and fear. Body reactions to those anxieties are often more readily noticed. Resisting contact or running away are more obvious than reactions to an anxiety about their own ideas or thoughts.

The death of a relative from a disease might cause a child to begin to imagine that a common bodily reaction, such as a skin spot or a rash indicates the presence of that disease. The child may dwell on that thought until it becomes a real fear and causes considerable anxiety. Monsters which emerge in dreams become a pre-occupying fear during the waking hours. Signals of inner anxieties might first reveal themselves by the mental signals described earlier.

Some anxieties protect children. For example, anxieties about heights, water and dangerous animals do this.

How do we know when a child's level of anxiety is 'reasonable' and needs reassurance or when it is becoming severe and needs clinical treatment?

Extreme fears and anxieties

Extreme fear reactions are referred to as phobias. Extreme anxiety reactions are called panic.

Phobias and panic reactions may, at some time or other, need the attention of a psychologist or a psychiatrist. (A psychologist is trained in the psychological study of normal and abnormal human behaviour; a psychiatrist is a doctor who specialises in the treatment of abnormal behaviour by the use of drugs, counselling and, more rarely, by surgery.)

How do we know when a child's fear and anxiety have reached a level requiring such specialist intervention? General guidelines for identifying behaviours which might create cause for concern are given under the heading 'Things to notice' in Chapter 10. Common fears usually do not persist; with time, they disappear, often without any adult or specialist help.

Specialist help should be sought for fears that persist for more than 24 months. Prompt attention should be sought for extreme anxiety reactions, such as dizziness and fainting, diarrhoea, involuntary urination and breathing difficulties.

A fear could be classified as a phobia if:

- a child goes to extremes to avoid the feared item;
- the child cannot be reassured by explanations and discussion;
- the anxiety response is beyond the child's control;
- fear reaction is 'over the top' and seems excessive in the circumstances;
- the child's reactions do nothing to ease the fear and might even make the situation worse;
- the fear is not common in children of his or her age;
- it persists for a long time.

(These criteria are based on those suggested by L. C. Miller, C. L. Barrett and E. Hampe, 1974, p.90.)

The Diagnostic and Statistical Manual of Mental Disorders (DSM) of the American Psychiatric Association defines three anxiety disorders of childhood:

- separation anxiety disorder;
- avoidant disorder (which focuses upon particular situations);
- over-anxious disorder, which applies to a number of situations.

Separation anxiety disorder

Separation anxiety means children become extremely anxious, sometimes to the point of panic if they are separated from someone they are attached to, or when they are separated from home or other surroundings where they feel at ease.

Children with separation anxiety worry considerably about being separated from a parent, guardian or other person lest that person is harmed or deserts them. Anything that causes them to be away from the person – such as attending play-group, nursery or school, even going to sleep – becomes a fear, causing the sorts of severe anxiety reactions mentioned earlier. They are also anxious about something happening to themselves (for example, being lost or killed).

Avoidant disorder

In an avoidant disorder, children older than 30 months show extreme avoidance of any contact with strangers. This will have been happening for more than six months. This behaviour socially disrupts relationships with children of their own age. At the same time, children seek warm affection and acceptance from their families and other people who are personally close to them.

Over-anxious disorder

Excessive and unrealistic worrying for at least six months about past behaviours, concern about progress in the present and about what might happen some time in the future, indicates an over-anxious disorder. The concern might be about school, their social group, sporting performance and so on. These children seek constant reassurance about their worries. They are noticeably self-conscious, easily embarrassed and made to feel silly. As a result of these anxieties they might complain of headaches, stomach aches, etc. and are very tense and unable to relax.

As with most behaviours that distress children, it is difficult to categorize types of anxiety. These problems are discussed in the book by Professors Morris and Kratochwill, included in suggestions for further reading at the end of this chapter.

The origins of children's fears

> The most widely held view is that children learn to fear.
>
> A minority view is that the biological attributes we inherit from our parents' genes predispose some children more than others to anxiety-proneness.

Among those who consider fears to be learned, some argue that the child is wrestling with a psychological problem which reveals itself in various fears and anxieties. Others think that fears are not necessarily linked to each other by a common cause but are behaviours which are learned separately, one by one in a particular situation.

As an example situation, imagine a boy who is frightened of dogs and of thunder and lightning. It could be that he was once bitten by a dog and on another occasion shared his mother's panic during an episode of thunder and lightning. On the other hand, it might be that the child suffers from a separation anxiety resulting from his parents' divorce. That might cause unrealistic and severe anxieties about anything that could separate him from the custodial parent. He might have developed a fear of these things because he imagines that if bitten by a dog he will have to go to hospital or that a lightning strike might kill his custodial parent. These fears are linked because they are both happenings which could separate him from that parent.

From this example, it can be seen that either or both views of how fears are learned could explain the origins of a child's fears or phobias and why they might cause anxiety or panic reactions. It is unwise to leap to either explanation without as much reliable, background information as possible about the child, his family and details of the fears and anxieties expressed.

Alleviating children's anxieties

If a child's fears and anxieties are excessively disrupting daily life, the child should be referred to a psychologist or psychiatrist for specialist help. This can be done by the child's family consulting their family doctor. Depending upon which view of causation the therapist holds, either:

- attempts will be made to find the underlying psychological problem to dispel the fears and the anxieties, or;
- the child will be helped to learn to become less frightened of the feared object(s) and to reduce the anxieties they cause.

Psychological health specialists sometimes use hypnosis to alleviate children's anxieties (Houghton, 1988).

Guidelines for everyday management of children's fears and anxieties

How can other professional workers in care and education agencies help to alleviate some of the less severe, everyday fears and anxieties of children in their care? Each child's fear needs to be treated uniquely. Therefore, only general preventive and management guidelines can be given here.

1. It is important for carers of children to control their own fears and anxieties; otherwise they give a model, an example which a child might copy (the child in the example above copied his mother's fear of lightning). Many parents have overcome their own fear of moths in order to enter a bedroom to capture one that is frightening one of their children. Therefore, provide a reassuring, calm example in the face of something children fear.
2. Discourage children's links with peers or adults who display fearful and excessively anxious behaviours because these can reinforce children's existing fears or teach them new ones.
3. Develop the habit of being calm and taking children's fears in your stride, otherwise you can give them an emphasis which children think justifies their concerns about them.

4 In your general behaviours, present a stable, calm model of yourself to children.
5 Never try to reduce children's anxieties by joking about them or mocking them because this can increase their insecurity and insult their self-esteem. It implies the child is fussing too much about trivial things.
6 Do not use words or actions which imply that children are in some way to blame for their fears.
7 Talk to the child and let the child talk about his or her fears. Be sure to listen carefully to, and to be thoughtful about, what is said. Otherwise, you might worsen the situation by implying that it is not important enough to warrant your serious attention.
8 Be attentive to what children say about their likes and dislikes. A dislike might turn out to be a fear or a phobia.
9 When appropriate opportunities arise, try to lessen children's fears by encouraging them to approach what they fear. This is called desensitizing and usually begins with the least threatening version of whatever is feared. A fear of dogs might start with a child being encouraged to watch and later handle different small animals (such as rabbits and hamsters), building up to watching and handling a small dog and later a dog similar to the feared one.
10 One way to start reducing a child's everyday fears would be to encourage the child to reproduce them in a painting, or roleplay the fears with puppets, or see a cartoon character discussing and managing the fear, and so on. This sometimes helps the child to feel in control. It can introduce humour into a situation, to defuse anxieties. If a child's anxiety can be reduced when faced with the feared item, the child has begun to conquer his or her fear towards it.
11 In the same way, a stable, calm carer helps to prevent children's fears by introducing them to the various people, animals, places and objects which are often feared. This could be done educationally, by means of a range of media and visits.

Key questions

Use these questions to check back over the material covered in the chapter and to assess your grasp of it, before moving on. Discuss the questions, and responses to them, with colleagues and tutors.

- In what ways do children signal that they are anxious?
- When might a fear be a phobia?
- How can children's anxieties be lessened by the ways adults behave?

Relevant S/NVQ Units

The material in this chapter will help with preparation for the following Child Care and Education S/NVQ Units: C4, C5, C6, E1, E2.

Further reading

Douglas, Jo (1989) *Behaviour Problems in Young Children*, London: Tavistock/ Routledge. Chapter 8 'Emotional problems' has a useful section headed 'Fears' (pp. 135–140) which gives examples of managing young children's fears.

Herbert, M. (1988) *Working with Children and their Families,* London: British Psychological Society and Routledge. Chapter 10 'More methods and techniques' has useful advice (on pp. 166–167 and 169–170) for helping children to overcome fears.

Morris, R.J. and Kratochwhill, T. R. (1983) *Treating Children's Fears and Phobias*, New York: Pergamon. This book covers all the issues concerning the identification, assessment and treatment of children's fears and anxieties. Overall, it is at an advanced undergraduate to postgraduate level, but the chapters on 'Introduction to children's fears and phobias' and 'Assessment of children's fears and phobias' could be managed by readers not yet at those levels. Chapter 2 'Diagnosis classification and incidence' gives a good account of the problems of trying to classify children's anxieties and offers some useful ideas to include in children's progress or observation records.

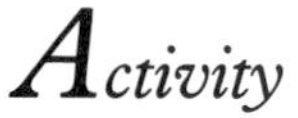

Chasing children's fears

Preparation
Read Chapter 5 carefully , especially 'Alleviating children's anxieties'.

Organization

1 Complete this activity on an individual or a group basis. Groups should have not more than five members. Individuals should omit steps marked with an asterisk (*).

2 Groups should:
- choose a leader,
- choose a person to record outcomes,
- allocate activities to groups.

1 Use three sheets of A4 paper. Write the heading 'people' at the top of one sheet, 'places' at top of another and 'objects' at the top of the third sheet.

2 Decide upon an age group or range you wish to focus upon, for example 3 to 5 year-olds, 6 to 8 year-olds, and so on.

3 Individually, using personal memories of childhood and experiences with children, list as many items as possible under each of these headings which are common fears for children in the chosen age group.

4* The group leader should ask each person in the group to read out first what they have written under 'people'. The recorder should note all the items mentioned by the first group member to contribute, then add to the list any items mentioned by subsequent members which are not in his cumulative list.

5* When this has been completed, the recorder should read out to the group the complete list of items under the heading 'people' and the group should make a note of them.

6 As an individual or a group, identify the three most commonly feared items in that list, entering 1 alongside the most feared, 2 against the next and 3 against the third item.

7 Procedures (4), (5) and (6) should be carried out for the headings 'places' and 'objects'.

8 Using these lists, pursue either or both of the following:
- Interview children in the chosen age group at your place of work or work practice placement to discover whether the group's lists reflect in actuality their everyday fears. Make a note of additional fears the children reveal. (Remember to obtain the permission and cooperation of the agency's senior member of staff and children's parents.)

- Focus upon the three greatest fears in one or more of the lists. Consider:
  - the possible origins of those fears;
  - how you might help to alleviate one or more in a child by a step-by-step desensitization programme.

Activity

Metaphor magic

This activity aims to allay children's fears through the media of storytelling, cartoons and painting.

Preparation
Read carefully chapter 5, especially 'Alleviating children's anxieties'.

Organization

1. Complete this activity on an individual or a group basis. Groups should have not more than five members.
2. Groups should:
   - choose a leader,
   - choose a person to record outcomes,
   - allocate activities to groups.

1. A metaphor is a word or expression for something to which it does not normally apply in its literal meaning. 'He's down in the dumps' expresses that the person's mood is depressed. 'Mr Sandman' personifies sleep because it conveys the sensation of eye grittiness that accompanies tiredness.
2. Using metaphors in stories, cartoons and other media can sometimes help children to grasp a message which adult explanations and discussions might fail to do as effectively.
3. Here are some suggestions. Develop one for individual use.

Storytelling

(a) Ask the children whether they like to listen to stories and whether they like stories written specially for them.
(b) Ask a child or group of children to tell you an everyday fear.
(c) Then ask the children to give a name to that fear (e.g. Mr Night, Mr Bite, etc.).
(d) Discover from the children their favourite, most fearless heroine/hero. (Television cartoons and stories, even advertisements will usually be the source of names suggested.) Be ready to suggest one or two if the children make only a few or unsuitable suggestions
(e) Prepare a story in which a child or group of children meets the feared person, place or thing together with their hero or heroine and are helped to conquer or overcome their fear. Remember to use the children's names in the story.
(f) The story could be illustrated. Draw the characters, cut suitable ones out of a mail-order catalogue or other source of photographs or pictures. A flannelgraph method could allow these to be used as a visual aid. (Stick some lint to the back of each cut-out or drawing so that they will adhere to a flannel or other suitable material pinned to a board for displaying to the children. In this way, the story can be built up more dramatically, as each character appears on the board.)

Cartoons

(a) Proceed as for (a)–(f) in the storytelling exercise and then reproduce your story as a cartoon strip.
(b) A method allowing for children to interact with the story is to structure the cartoon sequence so that the fears are overcome, but allow the children to write (or to tell you what to enter) in the speech bubbles of the cartoon characters. This personalizes it for them, giving a greater sense of control, an important aspect in overcoming fear and anxiety.

Painting

(a) Ask the child to draw and colour/paint her or his fear.
(b) On a separate sheet, the child should then be encouraged to draw what his or her anxiety looks like when he or she is faced with this fear.
(c) Ask the child whether there might be some famous person who could best help them to face and overcome this fear. (This might be a cartoon or television personality, a sportsperson or someone else known to a child.)
(d) Encourage the child to draw and colour herself or himself with this helper on another sheet of paper, showing how brave and strong the helper is.
(e) Ask the child to imagine this famous helper together with herself or himself meeting the feared person, entering the feared place or dealing with the feared animal or object.
(f) Suggest to the child that the helper gives her or him a special signal to show that the fear has been conquered.
(g) Ask the child to draw and paint how they conquered the fear together, showing how fear and anxiety look now that she/he has beaten them.

6
Aggressive children

Preview

This chapter deals with:

- children's aggressive reactions to frustrations;
- how children learn to be aggressive;
- levels of aggression in children;
- circumstances which promote aggression in children;
- children's copying of the behaviours of those they admire;
- ways to manage aggressive children;
- methods of changing aggressive behaviours.

The term 'aggressive' is often used loosely and it is important to be clear about its proper meaning. Behaviours are labelled aggressive when they threaten or cause psychological distress and physical injury to people and animals, or damage other living things and property. Sometimes a child's aggression is direct and intentional: he or she intends to hurt that person or to break the object. On other occasions, a child's aggression is indirect and less intentional, such as when a child knocks down another in the rush for one of the tricycles.

Causes of aggression

Aggressive behaviours have many origins. Sometimes they have a physiological or a neurological cause (brain damage, for example). Children with a tendency to irritability, which has a neurological or biochemical cause, learn to express it in a particular situation and towards a specific person or object. In other words, they learn when and where to express their irritability, just as other children do.

Frustration can lead to aggression in the form of temper tantrums. For example, young children can become very irritated when their limited skills and competence prevent them achieving their goal. We, as adults, understand when a young child flings the plastic nut across the room, having failed to screw it onto the toy bolt, exasperated by lack of skill. Adults do it too – it is from us that children learn some of their aggressive behaviours, by copying or modelling them.

Some situations are more likely to encourage frustration than others and are found to produce more aggressive behaviours in children. For example:

- demands upon children which call for understanding or competencies a child does not have;
- larger families can mean more brothers and sisters block the way to obtaining parents' attentions;
- being in a strange situation and not knowing the 'proper' ways to behave;
- any situation where children are not provided with the necessary information or tools to tackle the job in hand.

Such circumstances block children's goals and lead to feelings of frustration which may result in aggressive outbursts.

Whether aggressive behaviours stem from neurological impairment, from the biochemical action of hormones, from actions resulting from hereditary factors or from internal feelings of frustration, it is important to recognize that children *learn* when and where to be aggressive.

This is an important point. If most aggressive behaviours are learned, then it is possible for workers with young children to help them to unlearn those behaviours. To do this, we need to consider what encourages a child to repeat the behaviours, and why they seem so resistant to adults' attempts to curb them.

Learning to be aggressive

A particular type of behaviour will become more frequent when it is rewarded in some way, when it is reinforced.

Sometimes a child experiences reinforcement directly and immediately. This happens, for example, when a boy's physical attack on another child in order to obtain a toy or win an argument is praised and urged on by his friends. The aggressor is learning that such behaviours get him what he wants: the object or argument and the admiration of his friends.

In other circumstances, a child might learn by watching how children and adults behave towards each other. The young girl playing quietly in the home might see how her friend gains much attention from the adults when she has a temper tantrum and throws things. She observes how a particular adult solves the problem of a child disobediently handling the tape player by simply snatching it away and aggressively reprimanding the child. Without any of the risks of first chancing the behaviours herself, by just watching, she has learned ways of gaining attention or of obtaining objects quickly. This is known as vicarious learning – learning by means of observing others' behaviours, by noticing what pay-offs other people receive for behaving in particular ways.

Aggressive behaviour does not require any reinforcement from other people or circumstances because the very feeling of being aggressive might reinforce a child's own view of him or herself. A girl who has heard constantly from adults in her life, 'I'm tired of telling you to stop hitting your brother, you never stop; you are always hitting or fighting with someone' might enjoy a sense of consistency about herself if she continues those behaviours. She is behaving in ways people expect her to behave. (It was mentioned in Chapter 2 that people tend to behave consistently with their self-concept.)

> Aggression is common during children's pre-school years, typically decreases in the primary school but increases during early adolescence, and then declines again towards late adolescence.

Between two and five years of age, the wild, lashing-out behaviours of very young children begin to become more directed towards a particular person or object. As they get older, children are more able to use verbally aggressive behaviours instead of, or in addition to, physically aggressive behaviours. From about eight onwards, specific anti-social behaviours, such as lying and stealing, become more common.

Different levels of aggression

Children in pre-school groups are exposed to varying levels of aggression. Observations of three- and four-year-olds who were non-aggressive when they started nursery found that they soon became aggressive. Whenever a child successfully repels an aggressor by fighting back, that behaviour is reinforced. Parents will often advise children that the only way to cope with aggressors is to become more aggressive. How often are parents heard to tell a child, 'Go and hit him back'? When that stops the other child's hostility, it means that this child will use aggression again to change other people's behaviours.

Young children's aggressive behaviours can grow out of social interaction with their peers. Very aggressive three- and four-year-olds show high levels of social interaction. The more often young children mix with their peers, the greater the number of frustrating and conflicting situations they are likely to encounter.

If, by being aggressive they have got what they wanted, it is not surprising that their aggressive behaviours increase the more often they mix with others of their age. Observers have noticed three types of aggressive behaviour in nursery children:

- boys are more aggressive than girls in games;
- boys more commonly harass other children with threatening and teasing behaviours;
- hostility is used by both boys and girls to achieve a specific goal.

Research over many years at the Oregon Research Institute in the United States by G. R. Patterson and his colleagues included a study published in 1967 of four-year-olds who were observed continuously and reports of their behaviours dictated onto tape. They analysed 2583 acts of aggression and the sequel to each of them.

This research found that only children who were non-aggressive when they began at nursery and did not mix a great deal with other children showed virtually no increase in their aggressive behaviours there. Children who were in a more structured nursery setting – where teachers re-directed attention away from aggression – were less aggressive there than children in less structured settings. They noticed also that children who were very aggressive when they first started the nursery were like that for some months. It would seem that, even when children are put into a setting which discourages aggression, it takes time for aggressive habits already learned to lessen.

Promoting aggression in children

Patterson has written about the sorts of circumstances which maintain children's aggressive behaviours. Aggression towards brothers and sisters was much more common in families:

- where there was poor organization;
- where parents did not keep an eye on what their children were up to;
- where discipline was inconsistent and inappropriate;
- where positive attitudes towards others were not encouraged;
- where brothers and sisters got their own way by strong-arm tactics.

More recently, Patterson has noticed that aggression in pre-school children seems to be linked with depressive and irritable states in their mothers.

The aggressive, punitive methods of child-rearing which promote aggression in children are learned by parents from their parents; they are transmitted from one generation to the next. Children tend to copy or model the behaviours of people they are attached to or whom they admire – people referred to in psychology as 'significant others'. It is not surprising, therefore, that aggressive characteristics in parents are often copied or modelled by their children.

In the researches of John and Elizabeth Newson, begun some 30 years ago at Nottingham University, over 700 families were interviewed about their child-rearing practices for different ages of children. It was found that lower-social-class parents tended to be more aggressive and destructive; mothers in those families used physical punishments for their sons more than their daughters. Not surprisingly, lower-class boys showed more aggressive and destructive behaviours than girls.

If parents show intolerance and little affection towards their children and show no understanding about the need to explain and to discuss disciplinary matters, but rely primarily upon physical punishment as the means of asserting their wishes, their children are likely to model those behaviours when dealing with others.

> Children copy the behaviours of people they admire.

Community workers in family centres, playgroups, day nurseries, youth centres and teachers in schools become 'significant others' to children, important people in their lives. The behaviours of those adults are copied by children. A schoolteacher who is aggressive in attitude and behaviours towards pupils can encourage similar behaviours among them.

As might be expected, sports, film and television stars might also be significant people in some children's lives. Children can learn aggression from them. There is disagreement about the details of the effects of television upon children's levels of violence, but researches in both the USA and in the UK suggest that if pre-school children, in particular, watch a lot of violence on television, they are likely to display it in their behaviours. It is thought that they might be especially susceptible to learning behaviours by watching them.

In 1993, the murder by two ten-year-old boys of a two-year-old child, James Bulger, drew attention to the levels which aggression in children can reach. Significantly, it also revealed confusion among experts about what might have caused that aggression; some suggested a link with the aggression on television and in video 'nasties'. However, all agreed that more attention should be paid to the models of relationships within families and society which are presented to young children by the media. Young children more readily confuse reality and fiction.

It is important to understand what encourages aggressive behaviours in children because in longitudinal studies, which follow the development of groups of children from their early years to early adulthood, levels of aggressive behaviours were found to be almost as stable as levels of intelligence.

> Levels of aggression in individual children do not diminish over time but remain much the same.

Managing aggressive children

Many different ways to lessen aggressive behaviours in children have been experimented with. A common belief is that if children are allowed to give vent to their aggression, it will in some way burn itself out. In general, research has not found that releasing aggression by means of punchbags, so-called bobo dolls or even competitive sport for children has any significant or lasting effect upon the frequency of their aggressive behaviours.

Discussing with a child the factors which led to frustrated aggression can reduce it. Aggressive play, allowing a child to let off aggressive steam, can increase it.

An important consideration is to ask at what age children begin to understand their own emotions. Children start to use words which describe emotion around two years of age but apply them only to themselves. But children do not seem to begin to recognize internal, emotional states in others until after two and a half years of age. It is around five years of age that they show more understanding of other people's emotions and what causes them. Not until about 12 years of age can children understand mixed emotions, people experiencing more than a single emotion at a time. Older children are more likely to understand what causes an emotion. (Children's knowledge about the variables that affect their emotions is known as metacognition.) We might expect that with increasing understanding of emotions comes greater control over them.

> We should not expect the same degree of emotional control from younger children as we expect from older ones.

To help children to reduce their aggressive behaviours, it is necessary to reduce those factors which encourage them. The following list gives some examples.

1 Help children to develop coping skills, to be self-sufficient so that they are less likely to become frustrated and angered by a situation. This might include teaching them to think their way through a problem, training them in social skills such as communicating their needs and asserting themselves non-aggressively.

2 Discourage hostile attitudes and behaviours among parents and those who work with children. Adults should show that they can control aggression and that they have other ways of coping with frustrating experiences.
3 Do not allow children to gain by their aggressive behaviours; they must not learn that aggression will achieve their goals and get them what they want.
4 As far as possible, avoid giving attention to children who behave aggressively; that rewards their aggression and encourages it. Give praise and attention instead to increase those behaviours you want from the children.

Besides these general pointers which are aimed at promoting non-aggressive ways of coping, it is sometimes necessary to try to change children's hostile behaviours more directly. Usually, this is when the type and/or the amount of aggressive behaviours are severely disruptive, when one or more of the following methods might be tried.

Changing behaviours

Shaping behaviours

When a child shows unacceptably aggressive behaviours, remove him or her to a separate place for 'time out', a period of time during which nobody is to communicate with the child. She or he should be monitored there by an adult, to protect the child's physical and psychological safety. All adults working with the child must treat the child in the way that has been agreed.

As part of the same management plan, staff must decide which behaviours they wish to encourage in the child concerned. At first, staff might decide to reward a child for avoiding aggressive behaviours for a given length of time, from an hour through to a whole day. It is important to start with a short amount of time, which is within the child's capabilities. When the child succeeds, he or she is given a token (e.g. a star, or some plastic money).

The child should be able to exchange these tokens for something enjoyable. For example, perhaps the group will be going on an outing to the zoo. For each token, the child could colour in a segment on a cardboard snake. If all the segments have been coloured in before the zoo outing, the child will be allowed to join the group when it goes there.

Saturation

If a child shows hostility mainly towards a particular object, person or situation, then 'saturating' the child with that situation while helping him or her to cope with it can reduce that hostility. For example, a child who is anxious about being separated from a parent might display aggression towards that parent. That should not be allowed to prevent the separation because to do so would reinforce the child's aggressive control. Instead, the child (and the parent) should be helped to develop ways of coping with the separation (e.g. practising it, discussing it, phasing it) and, with supportive adult reassurance, to continue to be faced with the situation which provoked the aggression.

Family therapy
When unacceptable levels of aggression persist, the child and family could receive more intensive, specialist help from a family therapist. Child specialists, such as psychiatrists, psychologists and community psychiatric nurses, are able to help parents to manage hostility in their children. This kind of therapy involves watching families interact and, by means of small earphones, giving parents an audio link to the specialists, advising them about their behaviours towards their children.

Changing thoughts

Depending upon a child's understanding of his or her own and other's emotions, it is sometimes possible to encourage thought change rather than, or as well as, behaviour change.

Emotions such as anger are linked to particular perceptions and thoughts of a person. You feel angry when you think about how you have been treated or perceive the look on the other person's face. Therefore, if children can be helped to change the thoughts or perceptions that are leading to feelings of anger, they might display fewer aggressive behaviours. Here are some ways to attempt this:

- ***Self talk:*** Teach children to give themselves internal direction by talking to themselves. For example, 'He is only trying to make me angry, so I'm not going to let him annoy me – that makes me the winner!'
- ***Imaging:*** Children can be coached to imagine severe, unpleasant consequences for aggressive behaviours when they feel themselves becoming angry, or can be trained to imagine ways of reacting which would be more socially acceptable.
- ***Linking thoughts and behaviours:*** Older children can be taught how their thoughts and perceptions link with their angry feelings and aggressive behaviours. This is the basis of rational emotive therapy, devised by Albert Ellis, an American psychologist. We can learn to control a behaviour if we note what happened, what thought followed, what that thought made us feel and the response we made to the situation. By concentrating on changing the thought, it is possible to change the behaviours that follow on from it.

Key questions

Use these questions to check back over the material covered in the chapter and assess your grasp of it, before moving on. Discuss the questions, and responses to them, with colleagues and tutors.

- How do children become aggressive?
- What can be done to help children reduce their aggressive behaviours?

Relevant S/NVQ Units

The material in this chapter will help with preparation for the following Child Care and Education S/NVQs: C4, C5, C6, C7 and C9.

Further reading

Douglas, Jo. (1989) *Behaviour Problems in Young Children*, London: Tavistock/Routledge. Chapter 4 'Setting Limits' gives a straightforward account of the course of aggressive episodes in families and how to manage children's aggressive outbursts and temper tantrums.

Besag, Valerie E. (1989) *Bullies and Victims in Schools: A Guide to Understanding and Management*, Milton Keynes: Open University Press. Useful advice for parents and professionals about how to recognize signs that children are being bullied and how to implement a programme to protect them by preventing and reducing aggression by children towards other children.

Activity

Noticing children's aggression

Preparation
Read Chapter 6 and, in particular, the sections on 'Causes of aggression' and 'Learning to be aggressive'.

Organization
Individuals should omit steps marked with an asterisk (*). Groups should be no larger than five and should appoint a group coordinator.

1 Individually, write a list of the hostile behaviours you have seen children show – noting as many as you can remember.
2* Hand your list to the group coordinator.
3* The group coordinator should read out and write down the first list. Then the next list should be read out. If any behaviours in the second list are the same as the first, those behaviours on the first list should have a tick placed beside them. The coordinator should then add to the first list any behaviours from the second list which were not on it. This should be done with the list of each group member.
4* The coordinator should now have a checklist of all the behaviours mentioned by the group with ticks beside each behaviour to indicate how many group members mentioned it.
5 Devise a behaviour schedule which will have all the checklist behaviours down the left-hand side of a sheet of A4 paper and horizontal lines to form rows separating each behaviour. Leave some empty rows, to allow you to enter additional behaviours.
6 Use this basic schedule to observe the behaviours of a girl and a boy in your place of work or work-experience placement. Draw two vertical lines down your page and put the boy's name at the top of one and the girl's name at the top of the other.
7 You might find that you can only manage to watch one child at a time. Observe one child for an hour (or whatever time period the group decides upon) and then the other child for the same period.
8 Each time the child displays hostile behaviour, put a tick on one or more rows to record the behaviour(s).
9 At the end of the allotted time, compare what you saw with what you expected.
10* Next time the group meets, discuss the findings of each member.

Activity

Coping with aggressive children

The aim of this exercise is to consider ways of reducing children's aggressive behaviours by rewards.

Preparation
Read Chapter 6 and, in particular, the section 'Managing aggressive children'.

Organization
Groups should be no larger than five and should appoint a group coordinator.

1 Focus upon a particular hostile behaviour. In groups, a member could talk about an aggressive behaviour he or she wishes to reduce in a child at work. Alternatively, the behaviour mentioned most in the previous activity could be the focus.
2 Decide upon which behaviours should be rewarded in order to reduce the aggressive behaviour targeted.
3 Devise a token reinforcement system aimed at altering the child's behaviours. Use the suggestions given in Chapter 6 under the heading 'Changing behaviours'.
4 Remember that the system must allow the child to save up rewards towards some particular treat. Each time the child shows particular non-aggressive behaviours or desists from habitual hostile outbursts, a reward in the form of a token is given. These are collected up to a total that has been agreed with the child beforehand. When the child has reached that total, he or she receives the treat.
5 It is usually possible to provide a chart or some recording method which symbolizes the treat. This list provides a few examples to give you ideas.
   - A bus outing. A chart of a colourful bus could be made with ten windows in each of which the child draws a person for each reward. When all the seats are filled, the child goes on the outing.
   - A trip to the fire station. Depict a fire engine with a ladder with a firefighter on the bottom of ten rungs. The firefighter climbs a rung every time the child receives a reward. On reaching the top, the child visits the fire station.
   - A visit to a soccer game. A goalmouth has to have ten (reward) balls scored into it before a child can see his favourite team play.
6 The total number of rewards needed to receive the treat should be kept small from the outset. Otherwise, a child will tire of waiting and lose motivation to take part in the programme.
7 Use the programme to reduce the aggressive behaviours of a child in your care.

7

Right and wrong and children

Preview

Adults sometimes have to consider how much a child knows about right and wrong. This chapter considers:

- adults' influences upon children's awareness of right and wrong;
- how children of different ages show different degrees of moral understanding;
- the growth of moral behaviours towards each other;
- the emergence of a set of moral principles which guide behaviour;
- ways of promoting children's moral thinking and behaviour.

Awareness of right and wrong

Children's understanding of right and wrong is an important element in all the aspects of child care and education already discussed:

- the emergence of an ideal self-concept;
- the give and take of friendships with peers;
- relationships with adults;
- taking responsibility for aggressive actions;
- anxiety arising from behaviours which break conventions and rules.

Adults working with younger children sometimes feel frustrated when children seem blatantly to break rules and conventions. Adults might respond to that frustration by:

- 'laying down the law' and insisting that children do as they are told;
- trying to explain more clearly why a particular rule exists;
- punishing the children in some way;
- complaining to the children's parents;
- seeking the parents' help;
- or 'throwing in the towel', hoping that if ignored the children will sort it all out among themselves.

Mischief or misunderstanding?

Do children deliberately break the rules or is it that they can't understand or don't accept them? This question has been the subject of research continuously since studies at Stanford University in the USA at the turn of the century, yet it continues to puzzle those interested in child development. The question itself – and attempts to answer it – are not as simple as they might at first appear.

Children seem to develop from exhibiting a primarily self-seeking emphasis in relationships to having an awareness of the need to obey rules and to acknowledge other people's needs. In late adolescence and early adulthood, people develop attitudes and behaviours which grow out of a set of personal beliefs which show a greater consideration of others and their motives.

It seems that children at first rely upon adults to guide them about what is right and wrong but that later they develop their own set of beliefs which direct their attitudes and actions. If this is correct, then adults should take this into account in their relationships with children, especially adults involved in the professional care and education of children.

What do we know about how far children of different ages understand right from wrong? How do they reveal that understanding in their actions? We are all involved in moral thinking such as this: events in our daily lives require us to make moral judgements. We need to be aware of the differences between types of thinking about right and wrong shown by young children, and those shown by adults. In this way, we might better understand any mismatch between how adults see an event and how children see it. We might also recognize more readily the characteristics of child-like moral judgements in our adult attitudes and behaviours when they occur.

Mummy is always right

Researchers have consistently found that young children's moral thinking and behaviour is guided by what they think those in authority want from them.

Jean Piaget called this a morality of constraint: children adapt to prohibitions and sanctions handed down to them by adults. It is wrong to hit other children and grab their toys because mummy or the playgroup supervisor said so. Indeed, some adults respond to children's questioning of why they must behave in a particular way with the assertion, 'Because I said so.'

For young children, being good is the same as being obedient. Young children believe that the rules laid down by adults-in-charge should not be broken and, if they are, then some sort of punishment will follow for that wrongdoing. Because they do not understand all the implications behind rules, children don't see any need for the punishment to fit the crime. They would see no contradiction in an adult's yelling at them for shouting at other children.

Young children's games do not appear to follow any agreed rules. This basic lack of understanding of the purpose of rules showed itself when Piaget studied young children's actions and comments about playing marbles. It was really free play with marbles. When a little older, they copied the comments and actions of older children whom they had watched at play. But they still did not follow any rules.

When young children are told stories and then asked to make moral judgements about whether the events in them were either right or wrong, their replies are often interesting. Very young children consider it 'naughtier' to tell a lie to an adult such as a teacher than to lie to another child.

Young children ignore other people's intentions and seem to judge others' actions solely on the basis of the magnitude of the event. For example, a well-tried story describes one child breaking a number of cups accidentally, and another child smashing just one, but deliberately. Young children often focus upon the enormity of 15 broken cups compared with one, rather than on the lack of any malicious motive behind the first event and the deliberate intention in the second. Therefore, they tend to judge the first child to be more naughty than the second.

It is as though they do not grasp the principles of right and wrong motives. They might consider a big lie told unintentionally by a child to be much worse than a lesser lie told to deceive someone. The surface appearance of an event is noticed without taking into account all the factors involved. Ideas of justice show this same tendency.

For young children, the same disobedient action must receive exactly the same punishment, whether or not it was intentional.

Children also believe in instant justice. This is the belief that justice is some kind of abstract force which is inherent in nature and which immediately punishes any misbehaviour. For example, a girl who has fallen and cut her leg would be seen as being punished for having just told a lie to her carer.

Developing a sense of right and wrong

Pre-school children's behaviours suggest that they do what they are told is right because otherwise they will be punished. Piaget referred to this as a heteronomy, being ruled from outside oneself. Lawrence Kohlberg included this type of morality as part of what he called a 'pre-conventional' stage of moral development.

Norman Bull thinks young children live in a state of anomy, of lawlessness, responding not to order and rules but to their instincts and impulses. He noticed that during the early years of primary schooling this anomy gave way to heteronomy. He agreed with Kohlberg that when children begin to obey rules during the primary school years it is to satisfy their own needs by obtaining what they want or to avoid punishment by doing the right action.

Piaget considered that heteronomy – when children simply adhere to the rules imposed by others – hindered their growth in developing their own guiding set of beliefs. Bull suggested that it is only by learning that they *must* do something that they can begin one day to understand that they *ought* to do it. This means that usually young children will not question it when an adult insists upon some particular rule being obeyed. The children might not like the inconvenience of the rule or the manner in which it is enforced, but generally they do not appear to be able to question the morality behind it, or to disagree with the rule itself.

For young children, adults' rules must be obeyed simply because they are adults: it is the adult who is being obeyed more than the rule itself. To do otherwise might result in punishment, which might be physical or a withdrawal of affection.

In games, even when peers have agreed upon rules, young children ignore them. It appears that they do not grasp why we have rules.

Helping children to make moral judgements

This raises many questions about how we should manage young children. If they seem unable to grasp what rules are all about, is it acceptable for the adult to reply, 'Do it because I say so'? The answer to this depends upon why children show these misunderstandings about rules. Is it because adults don't spend enough time explaining why particular rules are necessary? Or do they not understand because their ability to reason is limited? Undoubtedly it has something to do with both of these factors, but just how much influence each has is unclear.

Sara Meadows (1986) points to evidence that:

- children develop greater social responsibility when they are included in family discussion;
- they show less social consideration when they are part of a group of children directed by an adult.

Young children have problems with moral questions because adults decide matters for them. This discourages them from thinking for themselves about whether something is right or wrong. They wait for adults to tell them.

Adults often fail to explain and neglect to give young children greater responsibility for decision-making. Young children's intellectual development makes it difficult for them to grasp explanations that are given. Those caring for young children must be aware that the children are not blameworthy for many of their actions. This does not mean that they are not accountable for what they do. It means that adults must not assume that children's misdemeanours are a premeditated breaking of moral, social or practical rules. Such behaviours are not 'bad' but rather a nuisance to adults' sense of fair play, order and safety.

> We should label the behaviour and not the child.

A statement such as: 'That is a dangerous or an unkind thing to do' puts the emphasis where it belongs, upon the action. The child's behaviour is not acceptable. 'You are a bad boy' inaccurately puts the emphasis upon the child's character. It suggests that the child is not acceptable. If, as just explained, this child is not deliberately breaking a rule and is not blameworthy, then he should not be labelled 'bad'.

> If we label a child as 'bad', we should not be surprised if he or she then fits this description, because we told the child that it is part of her or his character.

Taking account of others

There comes a stage when social acceptance in general becomes important for children. They respond to the praise and blame of people around them, not only that of adults but also of peers; not only those in their friendship or classroom groups but at the shops, the cinema or the sports centre. Obedience to the authority of a parent or other adult gives way to conforming with public opinion, with society's rules, with convention. Kohlberg called this the stage of conventional moral values.

This comes about with increasing age, as children become less dependent upon their parents and other adults for relationships. They value the relationships in their peer group, and discover how the members of the group are dependent upon one another. This results in a growing awareness of others and in feeling some responsibility towards them. Children begin to listen to what others are asking of them and to meet their expectations because they wish to fit in with society. This might be the small society of a school and neighbourhood, or society in its wider sense.

Bull used the term socionomy to describe the stage where a balance is struck between an awareness of oneself and one's own needs, as opposed to an awareness of others and their needs. As children begin to fit in with others, they receive praise, compliments and other rewards which increase their wish to respond to the requests of others.

They begin to keep to the rules of games when playing, but are so concerned to obey the rules that they regard them as unchangeable. During this phase, they still have no real understanding that rules are basically an agreement to cooperate with others both in small groups (such as a classroom) or in a large society (such as a nation). At this stage of moral development people are still self-centred. It is in a child's own interest to obey the rules because he or she gains praise from others by doing so.

This self-interest means that a person might break rules if others are not going to find out. Such a person still sees rules as constraints imposed by others, but considers that rules may be broken if it does not lead to unpleasant consequences.

Responding appropriately to different types of rules

Watch children playing and notice when one of them cheats. If the rest of the group fails to notice, the child might continue to cheat. The self-esteem that comes with winning is more important than keeping to the rules. Watch adults: they do the same. They feel concern about being found out not because a rule was broken, but because of the group's rejection. The rule is obeyed because it carries with it acceptance by the group. In some cases, however, acceptance by the group depends upon the individual's willingness to break the rules of the wider society.

> Acceptance by the group is more important than rules about behaviour.

Adults who are rigid and insensitive in how they apply conditions or rules in situations they share with children are reinforcing a morality of constraint. Children learn from them that rules can never be broken, even when they are hurting those who have to abide by them. Consider, for example, a rule that exists to protect children's safety: only staff are allowed in the kitchens. When a boy trips, injures himself and rushes for first-aid to the supervisor who is having a coffee break in the kitchen, he must not be told to leave because he is breaking the rule. That would make a nonsense of a rule whose principle is to protect the child's safety. Similarly, parents or a care agency might have a rule which forbids bullying, to teach children not to be aggressive towards one another. If a child is physically punished for breaking this rule, then the adult contradicts the very principle he or she is trying to teach the child, which is to avoid physical aggression towards each other.

Adults need to help children to realize that there are different types of rules. Practical rules, such as 'the plasticine must be put away in the plastic containers', can be changed. So can a conventional rule which arranges for boys and girls to have separate toilet facilities. But moral rules are not changeable in the same way because they are more universally applicable, irrespective of whether they are practical or conventional. For example, lying is wrong.

Adults working with children must examine their own attitudes towards rules and what counts as right and wrong. Careless comments and behaviours can confuse children who might be having difficulty in understanding what rules are about in the first place.

Towards the end of primary and the beginning of secondary school, children's thinking advances and they rely less upon a morality of constraint imposed by others. They develop relationships based on mutual respect. The give-and-take in children's peer groups teaches reciprocity, treating others as we would wish them to treat us.

The courage of conviction

As children enter adolescence, their ability to reason increases and they gain wider experience. They are able to develop a set of values which are held not out of fear of authority, or in search of social approval, but for their own sake.

Sometime during adolescence, a set of personal ideals is formed and a personal philosophy develops. Researchers tend to refer to this as a moral autonomy. A person becomes her or his own guide to standards and rules and no longer depends upon what others say is right or wrong. Bull suggests that there are three aspects to this autonomy or self-direction:

- emotional autonomy (from the family);
- value autonomy (from the family);
- behavioural autonomy (achieved when a person's actions match her or his beliefs).

Emotional autonomy

Those who are not emotionally free from their families might not be able to believe what they wish for fear of losing the family's affection. It is important to allow children to stand on their own feet emotionally, not to threaten the removal of love and affection simply because they challenge a belief or a convention.

Value autonomy

Emotional security allows young people to regroup their values, without fearing emotional rejection from parents or others for doing so. They work towards a consistency in their beliefs.

Behavioural autonomy
When a person is morally autonomous in this way, he or she is able to make moral decisions which are less influenced by fears of punishment or by what is socially acceptable. (Kohlberg calls these post-conventional moral values.) Fears and conventions might cause them not to act upon their beliefs. The important point is that their moral thinking is less dependent upon what others say. They know when their actions do not match their moral judgements. This means their behaviours are guided by their own moral principles.

Facilitating autonomy

How can adults, professional carers and educators help children to become autonomous or self-directing at the appropriate stage of their maturation? What might impede that progress? Some of the answers to these questions can be found elsewhere in this book, in discussions about empowering children's separation from parents (Chapter 1), the development of self-esteem (Chapter 2) and adults' recognition of children by the manner in which they communicate with them (Chapter 8).

Some general pointers might include the following:

- Help young children by explaining that some rules are changeable, while others are not. Be consistent but not rigid. Help children to notice that rules are for the benefit of people who create them.
- Encourage children to empathize with others who misbehave, to discover what the rule-breaker was thinking and feeling at the time. Ask children to consider what they might have done in the circumstances. In this way, encourage children to think about the feelings, motives and thoughts of wrongdoers – whether they could or should be held responsible for their actions.
- Give children the necessary information and responsibility for making choices when it is appropriate, so that they learn to think issues through, to weigh up the pros and cons of situations. Use pairs or groups of children to discuss how they might sort out a disagreement about toys or activities.

Key questions

Use these questions to check back over the material covered in this chapter and assess your grasp of it, before moving on. Discuss the questions, and responses to them, with colleagues and tutors.

- What phases or stages do children and adolescents go through before they develop their own moral principles and act in accordance with them?
- How can adults encourage children to decide for themselves what is right or wrong?

Relevant S/NVQ Units

The material in this chapter will help with preparation for the following Child Care and Education S/NVQ Units: C2, C4, C5, C6, C7 and C9.

Further reading

Smith, P.K. and Cowie, H. (1991) *Understanding Children's Development*, Oxford: Blackwell. Chapter 7, pp. 191–208. The sections 'Helping Others' and 'Moral Development' will give further information on Piaget and Kohlberg's studies of children.

Woolfson, R. (1989) *Understanding Your Child*, London: Faber. Chapter 16, pp. 138–147 gives a simple discussion of children's stealing, lying and swearing, and also of parents as models.

Telling tales about telling tales

The aim of this activity is to explore children's moral judgements by means of a story.

Preparation

Read Chapter 7 and, if possible, create an opportunity to tell a story to children. A tape recorder will be needed for this activity.

Organization

This activity is for individuals to complete.

1 Read the story below first to a pre-school child of three or four, then to a child of seven and lastly to a child aged 10.
2 Tape record your storytelling to the children and their replies to your questions because (a) you will not be able to remember it all later and (b) you will need to listen to the dialogue carefully in order to analyse it.

> This is a story about two sisters, Mary and Jane. One day, Mary saw the cat scratching its claws on the legs of the lovely new dining table. She rushed as fast as she could to tell her mother. Mary knew her mother was in the kitchen so she ran to the kitchen and pushed open the door. She didn't know that her mother was behind the door with a tray full of dishes which she was bringing to the dining room. When Mary pushed open the kitchen door she knocked the tray out of her mother's hands. All the dishes fell off the tray and smashed on the floor. Later, when her father asked her who had broken the dishes, Mary said that it was her mother.
>
> A few days later, Jane's friend called at the house to play. Jane asked her mother whether she could go with her friend to play in the park, but her mother said that it was too late, that Jane would be going to bed soon. So Jane's friend went away. Jane was very upset because she wanted so much to go to the park with her friend. She was so angry with her mother that when she went to the kitchen to get her drink and biscuit before going to bed, she took hold of a little cup that her mother had been given by granny when she was a little girl and smashed it on the floor. When Mary saw the broken cup on the kitchen floor, Jane told her that the cat had climbed onto the cupboard and knocked it down.

3 Ask each child the following questions:
   (a) Who was the naughtier, Mary or Jane, and why? (If the child says Mary was the naughtier, continue with questions (b)–(e). If the child says Jane, go to question (f))
   (b) Did Mary know her mother was behind the kitchen door?
   (c) Did she mean to knock all the dishes off the tray?
   (d) Did Jane mean to break the cup granny had given to her mother?

(e) So, again, who do you think was the naughtier, Mary or Jane?
(f) Is it naughtier to tell a lie to your brother or sister or to tell a lie to your mother or father?
(g) Is it naughtier to tell a lie to a friend at school (or playgroup/nursery) or to your teacher?

4 Listen to the tape and write an analysis of each child's replies, noting whether the children were able to consider the intentions of the children in the story or whether the focus is upon the quantity of broken crockery. What are the children's opinions about telling lies?
5 Compare your findings with what has been said about children's ideas about right and wrong in Chapter 7.

Activity

Children's values

The aim of this activity is to consider whether the values implied in rules made for children by adults are understood by the children to whom they apply.

Organization

- This activity is for individuals or groups of five or fewer.
- Appoint someone to record the group's deliberations.

1 Using three sheets of A4 paper, put the heading 'Moral' on one sheet, 'Conventional' on the next and 'Practical' on the third sheet.
2 Individuals or each group member should list the rules in her or his workplace or the work practice placement.
3 The group or the individual should decide which rules fit under which heading. The group's recorder should write them on the appropriate sheet of paper.
4 Consider each rule, whether it is mainly for the benefit of staff (S), for children (C) or for both (SC). Enter S, C or SC against each rule as appropriate.
5 Examine each set and ask which rules are absolutes (ab) and which are changeable (ch). Enter 'ab' or 'ch' beside the rules to indicate this.
6 Identify which rules seem complex and try to simplify them for children to understand.
7 Individually, question the children in your workplace or work practice placement about some of the rules there.
   - Do they understand them?
   - Which do they think are the more important rules?
   - Which do they think are the less important rules?
   - Are there any they would get rid of?
   - Why would they get rid of them?
   - Are there any they would change?
   - How would they change them ?
8 Consider whether the children's answers show any links with the outcome of the first part of this activity (1–7). For example, are the rules that the children don't understand the same ones as those you identified as complex? Are the rules which the children identify as more important those which you listed as mainly benefiting staff, children, or both?

8

Communicating with children

Preview

All our efforts for the care and education of children will be worthless unless we are able to communicate effectively with the children in our care. This chapter:

- describes why, how and what we communicate to children;
- suggests ways of using the different senses in order to communicate effectively with children;
- indicates how children's development and emotions affect how they interpret messages from adults;
- gives pointers for improving adults' understanding of what children say to them.

Communication with children

Communication is about sending messages to somebody or about receiving information from someone. The more we know about an individual's abilities to send and to receive messages, the better our chances of ensuring that those messages are clearly understood.

A person's senses are the channels used for communication. How effectively a person receives and sends information depends upon how well their senses are functioning and on their ability to use those senses. A more intelligent and literate person will usually be able to communicate better than a less able person.

How do we communicate?

Most people can use any or all of their five senses to receive information but they rely particularly upon their hearing and their sight. Adults communicating with children should take account of whether a child has the use of these key senses. Can he or she hear and see you clearly? To what extent is the child relying upon hearing, sight, touch or another sense to understand your message?

What should we say or do when we communicate?

To know what to say to a child, adults need to know something about the child's ability to understand and about any emotional experiences which might colour the child's understanding of what is communicated to her or to him.

- Has the child developed language? Can he or she talk and understand a number of words?
- How intelligent is the child? Can he or she understand your explanations easily?
- Might the child's emotional state or experiences in the past cause your message to be misinterpreted?

These same capabilities will determine how well a child can convey to adults what he or she wants them to understand.

Why do we wish to communicate?

Adults and children usually communicate with each other to give or to receive information, or both. What is going to be said and how to say it is influenced by why the adult or child wishes to communicate. If an adult is directing a child to do something, communication will probably be one way: from the adult to the child. The message is likely to be verbal and short. When a child complains forcibly to an adult, he or she may expect no reply to this one-way message. It will be short and conveyed in just a few words or even in actions (for example, by kicking or spitting). Adults and children learn more about each other when communication is a two-way conversation, involving both adult and child.

Even if we pay attention to the how, what and why of our communications, adults might not have the listening and questioning skills which allow them to understand fully and precisely what children are trying to tell them in their speech and gestures.

Channels of communication

Seeing (visual sense)

From birth, children use their sight when trying to make sense of the world around them. From a very early age, they are able to notice small differences in the appearance of things. For instance, for very young children, non-verbal information – such as a picture or gesture – is understood more easily than talk. Young children will attend to non-verbal cues from faces and bodies. They will be disturbed when what we say does not match the signals given by our physical appearance and behaviours. When holding a child, our voice might be saying reassuring words, but our tense body and frowning face could be telling a different story.

Children might be more interested in, and grasp more quickly, information presented in pictures. They are used to picturing stories and are more able to follow a message in pictures or cartoon style than in words. For example, young children might not understand the preposition in the sentence 'Rachel is beside a bed', but readily understand when shown a picture of Rachel beside a bed.

> Children will benefit from having words supported by appropriate actions or pictures.

Pamphlets and books written to help children with life events (parent separation, hospitalization, etc.) might be understood more easily if they have pictures illustrating the words. Many older children will be able to cope with information in printed form, but not all of them.

When talking to children about people and events in their lives, photographs of people and places can make communication more meaningful and more effective. When presented with a picture story which involves them, young children become more engaged with it if their own picture is included. Sometimes a video might prove more effective.

Much information can be conveyed to children in posters, charts and by a range of visual displays.

Hearing (auditory sense)

> Hearing what others tell us about ourselves influences our self-concepts.

What we hear is probably the most important influence upon our opinions about ourselves. To rephrase a World War Two poster, 'Careless talk costs psychological lives'. Most of us remember a psychological bit of us that was 'killed off' by insensitive, careless or deliberate comments by significant people in our lives: parents, brothers and sisters, friends, teachers, partners, and so on. Grunts, chuckles, sighs and other sounds can be as effective as words in our communications with children.

Most children enjoy music. Since ancient times it has been used therapeutically to affect people's moods – it still does this today. It can also educate. Do you remember the meteorological information in 'the North wind doth blow and we shall have snow' or the number learning in 'one man went to mow'? Songs can often get a message across to children when spoken information fails. This is worth remembering when we try to teach children about stranger danger, psychological and physical abuse, road traffic and the myriad other aspects of modern living which might threaten them. Children derive security from well-known stories, songs and sung rhymes.

From infancy onwards, sounds inform us. Adults should learn to use various sound forms, not just verbal messages, to communicate effectively with children.

Touching (tactile sense)

> Sensations of touch affect not only how children feel about a relationship; they also contribute to the development of their motor skills and intellectual abilities.

From birth, children explore by fingering and mouthing objects. The close touch of a mother during feeding time gives a baby feelings of security and other emotions. As children grow, parents and other family members convey acceptance or rejection of children by touch: hand-holding, hugging, pushing, and so on.

Adults should use children's tactile senses appropriately to communicate with them. Bodily contact (patting, stroking, tickling, etc.) is the most obvious, especially for emotional messages. The different textures of dolls, dressing-up clothes for fantasy play and social learning, clay and playdough all give particular messages through touch.

Other tactile experiences can give children a sense of competence, such as those involved in building jigsaws, puzzles and construction toys. Discovering the different feel of objects helps children to sort them. This ability to sort helps the development of their thinking.

Adults should endeavour to understand what they are conveying and what a child is trying to convey when touch is used in a particular way. Do both understand each others' meanings?

Moving (kinaesthetic sense)

Proprioceptors are sensors which send to our brains messages about movement in our muscles, tendons and joints. Inner-ear receptors tell us about head movements and the co-ordination of other body movements. These senses allow children to be aware of hand holding and squeezing, hugging, hair stroking; infants may be pacified by rocking and terrified by shaking.

As infants grow, the coordination of their body parts to achieve grosser movements (crawling, walking and running) and finer movements (manipulating a jigsaw piece, drawing with a crayon) give them a feeling of competence. The link between self-esteem and movement remains for many throughout life: witness the efforts put into sport and the pride of its achievements. We give messages to children in the activities and physical skills we involve them in. We reveal our thoughts about their competence when we do or don't allow children to try activities (climbing a ladder) or engage in games (encouraging children's swimming, soccer or gymnastics skills).

> For all children, messages from their senses have become linked with different experiences and the emotions associated with them.

A tight handgrip for one child is a sign of loving security, for another it is an aggressive, overpowering manacle. As adults we need to be aware what message we give to children when we communicate through their kinaesthetic senses.

Smelling (olfactory sense)

We can all think of smells which bring unhappy memories to mind and others which call forth happy ones. Many events in childhood have their 'olfactory label' attached. Obvious ones are children's anxiety at the smell of antiseptics in clinics because they have become associated with invasive medical procedures, or the reassuring smell of perfume associated with a parent's face when a child cuddles up on a lap for a story or receives a goodnight kiss.

> Emotions evoked by smells can be as powerful as any stimulated by any of the other senses.

Adults need to be sensitive to what different smells might mean to children in their care. Smells can provide a useful channel to communicate with children in diagnostic and therapeutic work. They can be used as a stimulus to evoke and explore memories and feelings.

Taste (gustatory sense)
From birth, children explore their environment by giving objects the 'taste test' – most things find their way to an infant's mouth sooner or later! Particular textures become associated with distinctive tastes. Do you remember sucking a pencil? Has it become linked with happy or sad feelings? If a teacher was reprimanding you while you sucked your pencil, perhaps the taste of it has unhappy memories for you. For young children, the soggy taste of a woollen blanket might be associated with security, because it is sucked for comfort in times of separation and loneliness.

Adults exploit the comfort provided by substitute nipples, knowing that dummy ones pacify infants and remind them of loving attention. Later, the taste of sweets is used to calm children's troubled emotions. (The part this might play in consolatory eating habits is an interesting question.) In such ways, adults communicate with children through taste.

Helping children to understand adults' communications

Acknowledge children's levels of development
Before children become physically able to explore, they will do so by looking at things, exploring them visually. With the growth of simple physical skills, children will first use gross motor actions to grasp things, put them in their mouth, bang them, and so on.

Very young children are more likely to understand what you are trying to communicate if you make use of the methods they use when making sense of the world around them. Adults should communicate with young children by giving them things to see or something to do, or both. Talk to them about what they are looking at or what they are doing. For example, a toddler will better understand what is being said when a video, photograph, picture cartoon or puppet display of a situation is shown at the same time.

Children from eight or nine years of age will follow some of the intricacies of a conversation or explanation, but young children need more than words alone. Therefore, encourage a child to communicate with you by talking together about a picture, while making a plasticine model, filling in speech bubbles on a cartoon character, finishing a story in a cartoon strip, talking 'through' a puppet . . . and so on. Your only limitation is your imagination.

Consider a child's emotional history
A child's emotional history and present emotional state might cause her or him to misinterpret an adult's way of communicating. A professional carer's relationship with an abused child could be marred by touch to such an extent that the child is unable to concentrate and will, therefore, miss the message a carer is giving. The child's emotional reaction to the touch could crowd out any important advice a professional carer might be trying to give.

When adults use ways of communicating which threaten children, communication between them will be blocked.

Confused emotions can cause confused thinking. (How well did you remember the facts when panicked by an unexpected examination question?) Emotionally disturbed children can benefit from non-threatening methods of questioning. A child could answer questions through the mouth of a puppet. This keeps a safe emotional and physical distance between adult and child. It allows a child to keep a 'secret' but it is okay for the puppet to divulge it. Similar ends are achieved by using cartoon or picture choices, ways of communicating with children which are familiar to them.

An adult's manner can encourage or discourage communication with children. Children can be put off by an adult's characteristics such as a loud voice, a particular accent, unclear speech or appearance (uniforms, white coats and formal suits). The situation as a whole must allow a child to feel at ease, free to talk. You might have to communicate with very young children via one of their parents because these youngsters need to adapt to a different voice and face; strangers' words might not be understood.

Adults need to know something about the development of children's use and understanding of spoken language. Crystal (1986) demonstrates how some children might misunderstand what an adult says because they haven't enough experience of the subtleties of the use of intonation in conversation. He refers to the findings of Cruttenden (1985), when 95 percent of adults – but only 45 percent of children – grasped the very subtle difference between 'She dressed, and fed the baby' and 'She dressed and fed the baby', when asked to match these spoken sentences with pictures.

The experiences of professional carers in talking and listening to children, and their knowledge of how children process language, show in how they frame questions for children. To help children to understand your questions, make use of non-verbal methods. If words are used, make them simple and use short sentences. When words are few and simple, the message is more straightforward.

Monologues or dialogues?

The reason for communication influences whether it becomes primarily one way, from adult to child or child to adult, or whether it is a two-way process between a child and an adult. Adults communicate with children:

- to control and direct them;
- to obtain information;
- to give information;
- to encourage children's imagination.

Children give roles to professional carers which influence the children's communications with their carers. For example, a playgroup or crèche worker might not converse with children, but only to talk to them in order to control and direct their behaviours. That person will find that children will develop a one-way relationship with her or him. The children will expect communication to travel only from the adult to the child and will not readily initiate conversation. This adult will not discover much from the children.

Understanding children's communications

Whether an adult understands what a child is trying to communicate will depend upon all the points made earlier in this chapter. Does the child in question suffer any sensory loss or impairment? What is the child's reasoning ability? Is the boy or girl laughing or crying when telling you something? What emotional effect is the message having upon the child? Is the topic of conversation causing a child to be too shy or too embarrassed to talk to you?

> When professional carers suffer sensory impairments, of vision and hearing in particular, a child's message might not be received in full.

Adults who can think clearly grasp what is behind a 'masked message'. They can read 'between the lines'. For example, children often hint at what they want to talk about. They first of all test the adult to find out how the adult will deal with what they want to say. How analytic is the adult's thinking: can he or she keep in mind all the possibilities thrown up by these disguised messages?

Children recognize the signs in a particular adult which suggest that trying to communicate with that person would be unsuccessful. When children discover this, they abandon the attempt. Watch children's reactions to adult visitors to their home. Children's behaviours indicate whether they feel a particular adult is someone they are able to talk to. These signs from children tell us whether they think we are interested in what they have to say.

When children think you are a listener, they will initiate conversations with you. If they know you are slow to criticize or difficult to shock, they will talk to you about anything and everything.

Unless an adult considers a child has a right to be heard properly and is genuinely interested in what a child has to say, he or she will not give the serious attention to children's communications which is essential for any effective hearing of the messages they are giving. Each of us has had experience of somebody's going through the motions of listening to something we are saying while not really hearing our message. We soon learn not to invest much time and effort in those monologues that masquerade as dialogues. Children do the same.

> Adults' ideas about children and their place in society are fundamental to the development of appropriate listening skills.

Sometimes, trying to understand how children and adults communicate makes a simple, everyday event like a conversation seem so complex. If we were to try to analyse how we walk, we might fall flat on our face. We all trip a few times before we learn to balance. Learning to communicate with children is much the same: dust yourself down after a less-than-perfect attempt and keep trying. Over a period of time you will learn what it takes and the responses of children will monitor your progress along the way.

Key questions

Use these questions to check back over the material covered in this chapter and to assess your grasp of it, before moving on. Discuss the questions, and your responses to them, with colleagues and tutors.

- How do non-verbal – compared with verbal – methods help adults in their efforts to communicate with children?
- Why are some adults better listeners for children than others?
- What enables children to be effective in communicating with adults?

Relevant S/NVQ Units

The material in this chapter will help with preparation for the following Child Care and Education S/NVQ Units: C2, C4, C5, C6, C9 and C11.

Further reading

Analyses of verbal communications between children and adults

Crystal, David (1986) *Listen to Your Child*, Harmondsworth: Penguin. This book gives a straightforward account of how children's language develops prior to starting school. It has many helpful examples of children's conversations.

Garvey, Catherine (1984) *Children's Talk*, London: Fontana. Chapter 6 describes how children use talk in social situations. Chapter 7 exemplifies how children learn about others from their voices.

Lindon, Jennie (1987) *Working with Young Children*, London: Hodder and Stoughton. Chapter 9 discusses communication between adults and children.

Using different media

For examples of how to use different media in order to communicate effectively with children, refer to any account of therapeutic work with children.

Axline, Virginia (1964) *Dibs: In Search of Self*, Harmondsworth: Penguin.

Activity

Smelling memories

Smells can be used to evoke and explore memories and feelings. This activity aims to give you some ideas about how you might begin to make use of smells in your work with children.

Preparation

Read Chapter 8 and particularly 'Channels of Communication'.

Organization

- Work individually or in small groups of no more than five members.
- Groups should choose someone to record the discussion.

1 Individuals: spend a few moments recollecting a significant, *negative* experience in your life to which distinctive smells are attached. It might relate to an object, person or place.
2 Do the same for a positive experience.
3 Consider how just recalling the smells can conjure up the experiences for you and how this might happen for children.
4 Decide upon two smells that would remind most children of an unpleasant experience and two smells that would remind them of something pleasant.
5 Discover whether or not you have guessed correctly, by asking some children which smells give them bad feelings and which smells give them good feelings.

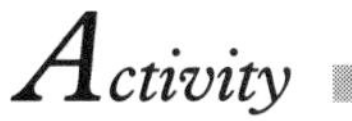

Planning to communicate with children

This activity should contribute to your ability to plan for structured interview techniques with children.

Organization

- Work individually or in small groups of no more than five members.
- Groups should choose someone to record the discussion.

1 Imagine you are going to be faced with trying to hold a dialogue with an individual child in order to elicit information from him or her.
2 Decide what it is you will be trying to find out from the child. For example, the child's feelings and thoughts:
   - about playgroup or day-care;
   - other children in general;
   - about particular children;
   - about adults in the care provision, or;
   - about a family event (death, hospitalization, new baby).
3 Consider which senses you could make best use of, bearing in mind:
   - the purpose of communicating;
   - the direction(s) of communication;
   - factors that will influence the child's interpretation of what you do and say;
   - that you will need to ensure as best you can that the child's communication with you is unambiguous, that you understand as clearly and as fully as possible the *essential message* he or she is intending to communicate to you.

9

Observing, recording and assessing

Preview

This chapter considers the observation and assessment of children. It includes:

- principles underlying observation and assessment;
- pointers concerning what we need to observe about children;
- a classification of the various techniques of observing;
- advice for achieving dependable records;
- a questioning of criteria for assessing children's progress;
- general guidelines for observing children's behaviours effectively.

Adults caring professionally for children are usually required to monitor their progress. Printed records giving details of children's progress are expected by employing authorities and by the children's parents.

Professionals in child care and education should be able to evaluate the standard forms and to cast a critical eye over record sheets which they are required to complete for children in their care. If the workers themselves are left to create their own forms for recording children's progress, they should be familiar with the first principles for observing and recording children's behaviours.

The whys and wherefores

Observing is part of our daily lives. Deliberately or not, we are constantly making observations and gathering information which we use to weigh people up and to develop attitudes towards them. Children often have no say in who is assigned to observe and assess them or how adults go about it. Therefore, we need to question the value of our observations and assessments of children. Information collected about children should be for the purpose of improving their physical, psychological and social wellbeing.

In order to help a child, we might need to know something about how he or she responds to the following circumstances:

- The environment or situation 'as a whole':
  - Is a child overwhelmed by a situation, whether it be a crèche, a community playgroup, a nursery school, or some similar care provision?
  - How does he or she behave in social situations: while shopping, visiting

friends and relatives, travelling in public or private transport, and so on?
- Various activities within that environment or situation:
  - In the crèche, playgroup or classroom, how does a child cope with particular activities and routines such as washing, refreshments time, changes in recreational activities, dressing, toileting, etc.?
- Other children:
  - How does a child relate to other children: to the same and opposite sexes, to peers, to older compared with younger children, to individuals compared with groups of children?
  - Does he or she readily join in small group games or does the child tend to be solitary?
- Adults:
  - Is the child at ease with both men and women in the care provision?
  - Is the child over dependent upon adults or a particular adult, or noticeably independent?
  - Does a child seek or shun adult company?
  - What are the child's behaviours towards the leader or supervisor of the provision compared with those towards the assistants?
  - How does a child react to separation from an adult carer when arriving at the playgroup, crèche, nursery school or other provision?
  - Does the child positively greet that carer when he or she returns to collect the child later?
  - What about adults not previously known to a child who visit the care provision: how does the child react to them?
- Particular aspects of a child or a group of children:
  - Does a child show gender-appropriate behaviours?
  - Does he or she display developed social skills in the situations mentioned above?
  - Is a child's cognitive development proceeding normally?
  - Is a child very active or withdrawn?
  - Is his or her appearance usually sad or cheerful?
  - Whatever the context, is a child normally contented or generally discontented, passive or aggressive?

Each and all of these pieces of information provide pieces of a child's personal jigsaw. Generally, the more pieces we have, the more completely we can view the child. But some pieces of a personal jigsaw might prove more important than others for understanding the whole person. Observations provide a factual account of behaviours or events which might offer answers to specific questions or a general appraisal of a child.

How should we observe?

Techniques

The techniques we use for observing can be:

- non-directed, noticing behaviours in a general way, or;

- directed, noticing behaviours which have been specified or identified in advance.

Non-directive techniques
These:

- are casual (i.e. observers watch when they have the opportunity and think it appropriate);
- do not follow closely a set of guidelines or plan of action;
- observe any behaviours;
- have a broad, general aim;
- resemble everyday, normal, child-watching activities.

Directive techniques
These:

- are systematic (e.g. observations are made on a timed basis);
- are structured (e.g. watch particular children and situations);
- target specific behaviours;
- have a precise aim;
- focus upon particular groups of behaviours or characteristics of children (their motor or social skills, language development, and so on).

Methods

The methods we use to gather information about general or specific behaviours might be:

- non-standardized, or;
- standardized.

Non-standardized methods
These:

- are informal (e.g. no particular procedure is followed);
- are unstructured (e.g. information is gathered in a haphazard way);
- might have had no trials to see whether the method works;
- allow the observer to interpret the information subjectively.

Standardized methods
These:

- are formal (e.g. a set procedure is followed);
- structured (e.g. a standard format is used to collect information);
- have been tried and tested;
- interpret information by means of a table of scores or other objective measure which compares a child's results with those of a sizeable number of other children or with the child's own behaviours which will have been systematically recorded on previous occasions.

The table on page 75 shows how our ways of observing and recording children's behaviours can be categorized.

The table shows that we can group observations into four types.

		TECHNIQUES	
		non-directive	directive
METHODS	non-standardized	ns + nd	ns + d
	standardized	s + nd	s + d

Non-standardized and non-directive
Professional carers frequently come to opinions about children by making casual observations of them playing in a playgroup, in the street, with their families, and so on. This is an example of a non-standardized, non-directive observation because:

- it is unsystematic – any behaviour might be watched;
- it is not carried out rigidly according to a set plan;
- there are no instructions for evaluating the observations.

Non-standardized but directive
A social worker or other community worker might have formed an opinion about the nature of a family's problem and be monitoring a particular group of behaviours, paying particular attention to behaviours at home, with father or in a peer group. Having collected this information, it is used as evidence to confirm or reject this opinion. Previous experiences with children and families are used to make sense of this information. This observation is:

- directive because it is systematic – a particular set of behaviours is being watched;
- directive because there is an overall plan to the observations;
- non-standardized because the social worker uses previous experience and intuition to make sense of what has been observed, rather than a table of scores or objective measures.

Standardized but non-directive
In establishments responsible for the care of children, records are necessary for monitoring their welfare. A professional carer might write for staff and parents a summary of a child's physical, psychological and social progress during the child's attendance there.

This is usually done by means of general, continuous observation throughout the length of a child's stay. Information about a child's ability to dress him- or herself is compared with guidelines provided by child specialists about what a child of a particular age might be expected to achieve in these skills. Other information about a child's skills in running, skipping, climbing and so on is checked against paediatric information about stages of motor development.

Such observations are non-directive because:

- observations are collected casually in the course of everyday work;
- they are not focused upon any particular aspects of a child's physical, psychological or social development or wellbeing;

but they are standardized because:

- the information is collected by a set procedure;
- it is recorded in a standard way;
- it is compared with some form of objective criterion (e.g. Mary Sheridan's charts of developmental progress, published by NFER-Nelson, 1975).

Standardized and directive

Sometimes, we observe specific behaviours in individual children or groups of children. We examine them objectively, for example, by comparing the results with a table of published scores. An obvious example would be a nursery schoolteacher wishing to discover a child's reading competence. She would need to know how a child compared with others of that age and whether the child's reading performance indicated that he or she had special educational needs.

This assessment of children would be standardized and directive because:

- every aspect of the procedure is carefully controlled;
- a particular set of instructions indicates precisely how the observations or test must be conducted;
- each child is given exactly the same task;
- a set amount of time may be allocated to each part of the task;
- the observations are interpreted objectively by comparing performances with a set of results obtained from a sample of children as similar as possible to the child being observed;
- as little as possible is left to chance and subjective interpretation.

To be sure of a reliable and valid way of assessing children's behaviours, we need to use commercially available tests and techniques. These are usually based upon scientific research. They give a reliable and valid method of observing or testing particular behaviours. The average professional caring team rarely has the expertise and/or the time and money to produce their own reliable and valid tests and techniques.

How dependable are our observations?

What do we mean when we say a technique or test gives reliable and valid observations or measures of a person's behaviours?

Reliability

This is a term used in everyday conversation and it has much the same meaning when used about measuring human behaviours. How reliable are the brakes on your car? Are you sure that they will always stop the car without fail when you press them? You need to be quite sure that they will consistently do this for you. Are you sure that the method you use to consider a particular behaviour in a child is as reliable? The consequence of an unreliable measure for a child's life could be just as serious as unreliable brakes for you!

To take an everyday example: when you use your kitchen scales, you expect the scales to read exactly the same weight each time you put a particular bag of sugar on them. You would expect a consistent answer from a child if you asked how many people were in his or her family.

> Ways of measuring should be reliable – they should give you the same result consistently.

Validity

Reliability and consistency are not enough. We need to know whether the way we are assessing a child is valid. What does this mean? What if you weigh an amount of flour on your kitchen scales and you are surprised at how heavy it is? You weigh it again. The machine records the same weight. In disbelief, you weigh the flour again. The machine consistently and reliably gives you precisely the same weight. You check the re-set mark on the machine to discover that someone has moved it and the beginning of the machine's measuring scale is in fact set at 3 grams. That caused a consistent and reliable overestimate of 3 grams on everything you measured. The reading is perfectly reliable, but the weight is invalid: the machine is reliably and consistently measuring inaccurately.

Think again about asking a child how many people are in his or her family. It might be a very reliable way of discovering whether or not he or she comes from a large family. But you could not use this information to conclude that the child was in some special need. That would be a totally invalid use of the information. Is there any proof that size of family is always linked with any special need such as neglect or abuse?

When we ask about the validity of a test or a technique, we are asking whether it is truly measuring what it claims to be measuring. We must know the limitations of whatever means we use to observe and draw conclusions about children. They need to be reliable and valid measures of whatever behaviour we are attempting to observe.

What do our observations tell us?

Professional carers often wish to know whether the behaviours of a child in their care are 'normal'. There are two ways by which we might try to sort out whether the children's behaviours we observe and record are normal.

- A nomothetic approach compares a child's behaviours with those which are normal for his or her peer group.
- An idiographic approach compares a child's behaviours with his or her own: those which for this particular child are normal or typical.

Nomothetic measurement

Standardized methods of recording behaviour often compare a child's behaviours with those of a large number of other children of the same age and sex as the child observed. They tell us whether the behaviours we have seen or measured are similar to, or very different from, those of other children.

A nomothetic approach evaluates a behaviour by first studying it in a large number of children to discover its most typical form. It then compares the behaviour in any particular child with the general norm or average for a large number of children similar to the child in question.

This approach tries to find general laws about human behaviour. An individual person is compared with the general population. We try to make sense of a child's behaviours or performance by looking at the norm or average for those behaviours in the general population and by judging how far a child differs from that norm.

Idiographic measurement

Finding that a child's behaviour is normal for the general population or some group within it still does not tell us whether it is a normal behaviour for this child. His or her pattern of behaviours is unique to the child. They are what makes him Michael or her Rebecca. This is an idiographic viewpoint. This tries to understand a child by studying all the behaviours typical of him or her. This approach attempts to identify what makes this person unique rather than how he or she compares with other children in general.

Who says you are normal?

There is a puzzle about what we mean by 'normal'. Imagine you are receiving tennis coaching to improve your moderate skills in the game. You feel satisfied with how your game is coming along as a result of the coaching. There are quite obvious improvements, but your coach says that your tennis is poor. Which is a more accurate picture of your behaviours: the observations of your coach or your self-observations?

It could be said that both observations are a fair assessment of your performance, depending upon what you are comparing it with. Your coach was comparing you with others and, on that basis, you were not making as good progress as the average or norm for your group. However, you were comparing your progress with the standard you had started with, against that criterion. You were interested to know whether you had learned particular skills you had set out to improve. Your coach was using a *norm-referenced* measure of your behaviours while you were using a *criterion-referenced* measure of those behaviours.

The comparison of a child's behaviours with the average for other children of the same age and sex is called a norm-referenced measure. The comparison of a child's behaviours with an agreed standard is called a criterion-referenced measure.

So, the same observations can have different meanings, depending upon how they are viewed. The feedback from your coach could have left you with low self-esteem and a resentful feeling of injustice, affecting your motivation to continue with the game. But what if the feedback had been a judgement about the sort of person you are (e.g. your personality)? Your feeling of injustice and resentment might be more devastating. Many of the judgements that carers make about children are of this latter kind and must be handled with great sensitivity.

It is crucial that professional carers are aware of how they are viewing the behaviours of children in their care. It is essential to be aware of the differences between norm-referenced and criterion-referenced judgements of a child's behaviours. We must weigh a need to compare a child with other children in general against a child's need for self-esteem and motivation. We need to know when an agreed set of behaviours for a child should be the criterion against which progress is evaluated. Should we expect children to achieve their own best or the best achieved by other children?

We could ask which approach tells us what we want to know about a child. Do we want to know how some particular aspect of his or her behaviour compares with that same behaviour across a lot of other children? Or do we want to know whether the child's present behaviour is consistent with behaviours which are typical of this child?

This shows that what counts as normal is relative – it depends how we want to use the word 'normal'. Imagine a situation where a child's behaviour is quite normal for his or her peer group. What if this child does not usually behave like that? Compared with the behaviour pattern of friends, the child is normal; compared to her or his own typical behaviours, the child is not behaving normally. You can probably think of a situation where your behaviour would be normal for the group you were in (a street gang, a student set, a school society, etc.) but would be thought to be uncharacteristic of you by those who know how you behave at other times.

So, which comparison is more likely to tell us whether a child is behaving normally? There is, of course, no single answer. The important thing is that carers should know what kind of assessment they are making on any particular occasion.

Who will use this information?

Legal requirements, professional needs and the desire to protect the welfare of children and their families, among other considerations, will influence not only how we go about the whole procedure of observation and assessment but also will determine who should have access to our findings. Taking into account why the information was collected, and how personal and confidential it might be, agencies need to decide a policy about who should see the results from the observations and assessments of its staff. Should it be:

- all staff or particular staff in an agency;
- other workers liaising with that agency;
- a child's schoolteacher;
- the children and families involved?

Some general guidelines

Here are some pointers for observing children.

- Know clearly what you want to observe.
- Decide upon the method and technique which best fit your purpose and the situation where observations are to be made.
- Preferably, record behaviours as they happen; otherwise record them as soon as possible afterwards.
- Record a factual description of a behaviour.

- Try to use a standard method when interpreting or evaluating it later. If this is not possible, be aware of the limitations to any subjective interpretation you record.
- Be aware of the consequences to children of using:
  - nomothetic or idiographic measurement;
  - reliable and valid observations or measures;
  - norm- or criterion-referenced comparisons.
- Decide who should have access to the information and evaluation arising out of your observations and assessments.

Key questions

Use these questions to check back over the material covered in this chapter and assess your grasp of it, before moving on. Discuss the questions, and responses to them, with colleagues and tutors.

- What do we need to know about a child before we can make sense of any observation and record of the child's behaviours and developmental progress?
- What are the advantages and disadvantages of the different techniques and methods we can use to observe children?
- Is it more helpful to know how a child's behaviours and progress compare with those of children of the same age and sex, or to know how much they differ from the child's own, usual ways of behaving?
- Why is it important to know whether observations and records of children are reliable and valid?

Relevant S/NVQ Units

The material in this chapter will help with preparation for the following Child Care and Education S/NVQ Units: C2, C4, C5, C6, C10, C16 and M8.

Further reading

Lindon, Jennie (1987) *Working with Young Children*, London: Hodder & Stoughton. Part 1: 'The value of observation and planning in work with young children'.

Ollendick, T. H. and Hersen, M.(1984) *Child Behavioural Assessment*, New York: Pergamon. Discusses general principles of assessment and includes appraisals of standardized instruments which are available commercially.

Pellegrini. A.D. (1987) *Applied Child Study: A Developmental Approach*, Hillsdale, New Jersey: Lawrence Erlbaum. Chapter 4 'The use of tests', Chapter 6 'Naturalistic approaches' and Chapter 8 'Children's social competence': these take further issues raised in this chapter.

Sylva, K., Roy, C. and Painter, M. (1986) *Child watching at Playgroup and Nursery School*, Oxford: Basil Blackwell. An account of the analysing of hundreds of hours of observation of children under five as part of the Oxford Pre-school Project. It describes how it went about the task and the inferences to be drawn from the findings.

Activity

Techniques for observing and assessing children

Organization
For completion by individuals or small groups of five or fewer.

1 Individually or as a group, write two lists of children's behaviours or attributes which you think are worth noting:
(a) those which children show frequently when in groups;
(b) others which are not very common.
2 Design and print a record sheet for observing and recording behaviours in (a) or (b), paying attention to the general guidelines given in this chapter.
3 Consider how you might use this as the basis for observing and/or asessing the behaviours of a single child or a group of children.
4 Write an outline of what you expect to be its strengths and weaknesses.
5 Conduct a pilot test of the instrument you have designed.
6 As a group or individually, study the results of this pilot test.

Keeping records of children's progress

Organization
For completion by individuals or small groups of five or fewer. Groups should appoint recorders.

1 Obtain a copy of any commercially available observation schedule, rating scale or assessment of personality, intelligence, attainment, etc. The following list gives examples of publications by NFER-Nelson (you might need to ask a health service worker such as a health visitor or psychologist to show you one of these, as they can be expensive to purchase):
   - The Portage Early Education Programme: Checklist;
   - Pre-school Behaviour Checklist;
   - Special Needs Assessment Software – CDT and VCT Tests;
   - Raven's Coloured Progressive Matrices.
2 Write a description of it to include:
   - what it claims to measure;
   - whether it uses a directive or non-directive technique to gather information;
   - any information its manual offers about its reliability and validity;
   - whether it uses a standardized or non-standardized method to evaluate the information it collects;
   - whether it is mainly nomothetic or idiographic,
   - the extent to which it is norm- or criterion-referenced.
3 Use it to record the behaviours of one or more children.
   - Write a short account of what it was like to use and how useful its information might be.

10

Watching children play

Preview

This chapter gives:

- general guidelines for deciding whether a child's play activities indicate the need for specialist help;
- descriptions of some developmental and behavioural disorders of childhood;
- indicators of how these disorders might be revealed in their play activities;
- suggestions for creating a play environment for diagnostic purposes.

Play – a window into children's lives

If there is one aspect of working with children about which there appears to be universal agreement it is the value of play.

Why all the fuss about play? Does this just mean children 'playing around' – like they do on the street, for instance? What's special about play?

Play can be 're-creation', both emotionally and intellectually. For everyone, play can be a way of escaping from the pressures of more formal learning. Young children have been exploring their world through their senses from the moment they were born. Through explorations such as watching, touching, smelling and sucking, they begin to learn about everyday life. As children begin to walk and talk, their explorations become more ambitious, more adventurous and more complex.

Much of children's early discovery includes copying adults, trying out what they see their parents and other adults doing, finding out how something works, communicating with other children, enjoying the touch of different textures, hearing different sounds, feeling the movements of running, jumping, and so on. Adults have loosely regarded this as 'just play', when it is also the natural and pleasurable way children learn by exploring and discovering.

> Because play is the natural and pleasant way for children to learn, it makes sense to use it for their physical, intellectual, emotional and social education.

A number of writers offer accounts of how normal physical and intellectual development is revealed in play activities (see Matterson, 1989 and Garvey, 1977 for example). The focus here is upon using play as a means of identifying and diagnosing developmental and behavioural disorders.

Professional carers need to observe carefully what children do and say in order to notice signals which might indicate something amiss in a child's development. Adults working with children, especially young children, could play a valuable role in helping families to prevent problems arising in the care and education of their children. Child-care and education workers could advise parents about appropriate specialist guidance when necessary and offer other caring advice and skills themselves.

Watching children play involves joining them in their activities. Much social research involves participant observation. The watching suggested here is of that nature: joining children in their play, but being professionally watchful and alert at the same time. This means being aware of how a child reacts both in one-to-one relationships with an adult or another child, and in social groups of two or more adults or children. Watchful carers also pay attention to a child's behaviours when he or she is playing alone.

Things to notice

General guidelines for identifying whether any particular child's behaviours should give cause for concern would include the following:

- degree of deviance;
- frequency;
- quality;
- duration;
- consequences;
- reality base;
- overall effect.

Degree of deviance

How different is the child's behaviour from ordinary or normal children of the same age and gender?

Frequency

How often does the child display the behaviour you are concerned about?

Quality

How severe or intense is the behaviour? Many children will at some time rock themselves, twist their hair, or bang their head deliberately and rhythmically against something. But you would not expect children to engage in this behaviour to the extent that they withdraw into a personal cocoon, lose hair or cause severe self-bruising.

Duration

Is the behaviour transitory or enduring? Is it acute? For example, did the behaviour occur only during a dramatic life event such as a family change, like the birth of a brother or sister? Is it chronic? For instance, does a child show repetitive behaviours, constantly drawing a particular person or object and in the same colours, etc.?

Consequences
How much disruption does the behaviour cause to the child, his or her parents and to other people?

Reality base
To what extent is the child still in touch with reality? Many children at some time or another engage in speaking a 'silly' language. They might enjoy daydreaming and lose themselves in their own private world. Sometimes they react differently in their relationships with adults and children. But usually children do not lose touch with reality: they return to ordinary behaviour when their fantasy behaviours are interrupted by meal breaks or friends suggesting a different game.

Overall effect
Is the behaviour stopping the child or parents from leading a normal life?

Besides these general pointers, some behaviours can be particularly characteristic of psychological or physical problems in children. Keep the guidelines above in mind when reading about behaviours typical of particular psychological or physical difficulties of children. Many children will show some of these behaviours, but the decision whether to seek specialist advice depends upon the answers to the questions posed in these guidelines.

The guidelines and the descriptions of particular psychological and physical special-need profiles that follow could be used to decide whether to seek the guidance of a specialist: an educational or clinical psychologist, a social worker, a health visitor, or any other professional concerned with the care and education of children.

Play and problem behaviours

Maladaptive children, as the label suggests, have difficulty in adapting their behaviours in order to fit into a group. In general, maladaptive behaviours reveal themselves in excesses: an excess of inhibition or an excess of aggression.

Inhibited children

In play, chronically inhibited children will:

- be unspontaneous towards other people or toys, or about having to play in open, unstructured spaces;
- show no real delight, excitement or enjoyment in their play activities;
- be over-careful with toys (for example, toys would more often than not be returned carefully to their proper place);
- find their play environment is a bewildering threat;
- stay close to adults, asking permission for everything;
- sometimes try to ingratiate themselves with staff members;
- appear to be unhappy with themselves;
- deprecate things around them. Toys are described as dirty and other children as smelly, for example. They can be over-concerned with distancing themselves from what they judge to be dirty.

Aggressive children

In contrast, children whose maladaptive behaviours are very aggressive try to dominate the playing group. Aggressive children may:

- exploit other children, shoving them around, claiming toys and territory are theirs and not for sharing with others.
- play in a sadistic way, breaking toys, being preoccupied with weapons or enjoying creating pain or unhappiness in peers and adults by their play;
- reject aggressively any limits such as rules or other restrictions introduced by care workers to curb anti-social or physically threatening behaviours;
- often blame someone else when challenged about damaged property or hurt children.

Abused children

The abuse of children is nothing new: it has been a characteristic of many societies for centuries. On the other hand, legal attempts to protect children from maltreatment by societies and by individuals is comparatively recent. Professional carers need to be alert to aspects of children's behaviours and attitudes which might indicate abuse. This topic is dealt with in Chapter 13, where definitions of abuse and a more comprehensive list of indicators of abuse are discussed. This chapter focuses on signs that are most likely to reveal themselves in play behaviours and in interactions with carers.

Indicators of physical, emotional or sexual abuse

Children who are being abused might show some of the following behaviours in their play activities. In themselves, such behaviours are never proof of abuse by others, but indicate that carers should keep a watchful eye on a child who displays them. The type of abuse which the behaviour might indicate is indicated in square brackets.

- In play, human interaction is avoided; the child prefers to play with objects rather than people. [Failure to thrive/emotional abuse.]
- A child is inactive and apathetic compared with her or his peers. [Failure to thrive/emotional abuse.]
- A child shows little tendency to explore her or his environment, despite being mentally alert to what is going on around them. [Failure to thrive/emotional abuse.]
- Play is immature, associating more with younger children, and avoiding the challenges of games with peers. [Failure to thrive can mean delay in physical and emotional development and an inability to meet the physical demands of age-mates.]
- A child avoids slides or sitting at an activity for any length of time. [Physical abuse causes bruising to the lower back and buttocks.]
- Inability to join in games owing to soreness or wounds. [Physical abuse.]
- A child displays low self-esteem, shows no initiative and expresses a poor opinion about herself or himself. [Physical and/or emotional abuse.]
- A child might show self-aggression, physically hurting and insulting herself or himself in play activities. [Physical and/or emotional abuse.]

- Play shows aggression towards toy objects (e.g. doll families), professional carers and/or other children. [Physical, sexual and/or emotional abuse.]
- A child is preoccupied with bedrooms, bathrooms or toilets in doll's house play. [Sexual abuse.]
- A wary watchfulness and reluctance to engage in close play with adults. [Sexual abuse.]
- Knowledge of sexual behaviours beyond their age in drawings and paintings and in doll play. [Sexual abuse.]

If a child's behaviours cause concern, bring them to the attention of a health visitor or social worker.

Brain damage and hyperactivity

If there is a record of proven brain damage, generally parents tell care workers. Sometimes, children might have to wear protective headgear in such cases. Children with proven brain damage of any severity more usually receive special educational provision and would not be placed in ordinary educational or care provision. There is evidence that children with brain damage (for example, cerebral palsy and epilepsy) are more likely than ordinary children to show behaviour disturbances seen in psychological and psychiatric disorders.

Behaviours indicating brain damage

When there is no observable damage to the brain, sometimes a particular pattern (or syndrome) of behaviours raises the possibility of there being some level of brain dysfunction. Some paediatric neurologists believe that slight brain damage might show itself in the ways children think and behave, even when the usual signs of brain damage are not observable. This does not mean that a child displaying such behaviours is necessarily brain damaged.

Children displaying hyperactivity are constantly on the move; they are abnormally restless and overactive. Hyperactivity is the behaviour commonly linked with brain damage in everyday discussion, although there is no neurological proof that the two are linked. Also, not all children with proven brain damage show hyperactive behaviour. There is disagreement about the characteristics of this kind of hyperactivity because they often overlap with the overactivity found in unsocialized conduct disorders, when children have not learned to behave in ways which are acceptable to adults and other children.

Some hyperactive children display a particular syndrome. This was labelled 'minimal brain dysfunction' in 1947 by Strauss, a paediatric neurologist, and his colleague Lehtinen. Today the term hyperkinetic syndrome is used because it emphasizes the pattern of behaviours. The earlier term implied an underlying brain damage which has not yet been proven.

Hyperkinetic behaviours

The hyperkinetic syndrome describes children who tend to have little focus, to be 'on the go', restlessly switching from one activity to another. Some experts believe that this results from their being easily distracted. Recent research suggests that it might be due to difficulties in sustaining attention, being unable to concentrate for any length of time.

The American Psychiatric Association in its *Diagnostic and Statistical Manual of Mental Disorders* (third edition revised) refers to 'attention-deficit hyperactivity disorder'. Attention means being able to focus closely on something in particular, to plan and to be systematic when investigating how to assemble a jigsaw or a construction toy and to do this for some length of time without being too easily distracted from the task in hand. An attention-deficit disorder indicates that a child displays considerable difficulty with these sorts of activity. This often shows itself before seven years of age.

Play indicators

In play, hyperkinetic children:

- tend not to persist with any particular activity owing to their having difficulty in concentrating other than for a short attention span;
- have no particular goal, but give toys and equipment only passing attention, moving from one activity to another without completing any of them;
- tend to be impulsive, unable to hold back from bursting into other children's play inappropriately or chattering excessively and interrupting conversations;
- may endanger themselves by launching into some action without seeming to realize the consequences to self or others;
- can be chaotic and disorganized, a mixture of all these behaviours.

Children with brain damage, especially cerebral palsy, might show one or more of the following signs in play activities:

- poor motor control: a clumsy gait, poor coordination when walking or in fine finger activities such as holding a crayon or screwing a large plastic nut on to its bolt;
- losing orientation in space: when climbing, dancing or jumping they might consistently lose their balance and bump into things or knock them over;
- involuntary behaviours: muscle twitching, contortions, or impulsive and inconsequential behaviours which ignore the problems they cause.

Play activities for children whose brain damage causes mental handicap will show behaviours different from their age-mates.

- Social behaviours are noticeably different from that which might be expected for their age. For example, smiling and laughing develop later than usual in children with Down's Syndrome (the most common form of mental handicap which in 1959 was found to be caused by an abnormality in chromosomes at conception).
- Interactions within families show that, because of delays in development, less is expected of mentally handicapped than ordinary children by members of their families.
- Problems in adapting to social demands occur because of delays in development and brain damage.

Pervasive development disorders

Doctors and psychologists concerned with children's development have noticed that some severe mental disorders first reveal themselves during infancy (often before 30 months of age) or early childhood (up to three or four years of age).

Infantile autism is typical of this disorder. It usually reveals itself before 30 months.
Children with autism behave differently from other children:

- in their use of language;
- in their social relationships;
- in their characteristic play activities.

The development of speech is delayed and when communication emerges it bears distinctive features:

- often there is no imitation of social speech and signals, such as waving 'bye-bye';
- pronouns might be reversed: 'You want a drink' is used to mean 'I want a drink';
- an adult's words or phrases might be repeated parrot-like (referred to as echolalia);
- understanding what others say can be delayed or impaired;
- speech might be in a monotone, with a 'flat' delivery, with no meaningful facial or head movements;
- communication generally is affected (autistic children might signal what they want by grasping an adult's wrist and taking them to the object);
- pointing might be with the whole hand rather than with a finger.

There are many ideas about why children with autism show difficulties of understanding communications from others. Research seems to point to their having a difficulty in processing the information received by their senses. Autistic children have problems in understanding social relationships. They have difficulty in responding to social cues.

- They do not sympathize with other people's feelings.
- They fail to 'give and take' in social situations.
- They do not go to parents for comfort or show any sign of welcome when parents return after an absence.
- They are content to be isolated and not to relate to other children (for example, in cooperative play).
- They fail to make personal friendships.

It was once assumed that social anxiety caused autistic children to avoid mixing with others, but research has shown that they respond when others begin social contact with them. Some experts in the study of autism conclude that it is the reciprocity, the give-and-take of communication, that causes avoidance of social interaction. It is as though autistic children do not understand emotions: they have been found to recognize themselves in a mirror but to show no emotional reaction to this view of themselves.

Play indicators

As might be imagined, all this reveals itself in the play of autistic children.

- They do not show the sort of creative and imaginative play engaged in by other children.
- One object is not used to represent another, for example a box is not used imaginatively as a substitute for a car or a house.
- Play tends to be repetitive, rigid and limited – for example, a child with autism might monotonously line up objects in rows.

- They seem preoccupied with sameness and will object strongly if anyone intervenes to encourage more meaningful play.
- Play seems to have no purpose.
- Autistic children can show a fascination with unusual characteristics of objects such as their smell or feel and can become very attached to things (for example, a particular wooden bead).
- The same intenseness shows in repetitious motor behaviours: for example, the adept twirling of a shiny round lid on the same spot in a rigid routine, or rapid finger movements near their eyes.
- Autistic children have difficulty in imitating actions in the usual miming games enjoyed by children.

Children with autistic difficulties have been helped by learning environments which have clear routines, well-structured programmes with simple, direct interaction with carers, rather than those which have open and casual, do-as-you-please routines.

Listening to language

When watching or joining-in children's play, it is important to pay attention to their talking and listening. There are two basic categories for organizing observations of children's language, whether a child has difficulties in receiving information or in expressing it. Notice whether any child shows:

- a receptive language difficulty: is he or she understanding what is said?
- an expressive problem: can a child make himself or herself understood by others?

Specific language impairment

Children's spoken language might be slow to develop for a number of reasons:

- a deprived environment;
- a psychological disturbance;
- a hearing loss;
- an impaired muscle tone in the muscles of the tongue, lips, soft palate or larynx;
- mental handicap.

Children who have a hearing loss receive unclear speech sounds and therefore speak them inaccurately. Sometimes they fail to understand what is being said because they do not hear the full word. They might not respond if they are not looking at the speaker's face because they have not noticed that they are being spoken to. Children with a high-frequency hearing loss might appear to hear reasonably well, but could fail to hear accurately when there is a lot of background noise.

Some language disorders cannot be explained in any of these ways, and are called specific language impairments. Children with those impairments find it difficult to store and reorganize what they hear, especially spoken information, even though they might be intellectually average or above average in other aspects of their development. These children usually have difficulty expressing themselves verbally, even though their hearing and understanding of speech seems all right.

Play indicators

Specific language impairment could show itself during play in a child's mis-use of language, which might include the following types of error in their speech:

- when trying to repeat questions or negative statements, they jumble the words ('what is he doing?' might become 'what he do?', 'You mustn't say that' could become 'you no say');
- articulation errors, the unclear speech found in young children, can persist after four to five years of age;
- omissions ('gree' for 'green');
- substitutions ('embelofe' for 'envelope');
- transpositions ('aminal' for 'animal');
- inaccurate sequencing of consonants ('bilikses' for 'bicycle') can be heard in their speech.

Checking speech and language

When watching children at play, here are some useful tips to help you to decide whether a child needs specialized professional attention for his or her speech. If in doubt, seek the advice of a speech therapist or other appropriate health professional.

1. Check whether the child is responding to everyday sounds.
2. Does he or she respond to someone's speech when that person is out of view?
3. When facing the child, can the child follow your conversation when you hide your lips by holding your hand in front of your mouth? (Hearing-impaired children might be relying upon lip-reading.)
4. How does the child communicate his or her needs? Is speech avoided?
5. How do members of the family communicate with the child, mainly by speech or mainly by gesture?
6. For what periods of time does the child play alone? (Children with language difficulties sometimes avoid social situations.)
7. Can the child understand simple instructions easily?
8. Can the child understand more complicated requests?
9. Is the quality of the child's voice very different from most other children in the group. Does it have a hoarse or nasal quality?
10. Does the child's speech flow or is stammering common?
11. Can you understand more than about one fifth of what the child says?

A play environment for general diagnostic purposes

To provide diagnostic opportunities, play equipment and activities must allow for children to express the range of behaviours mentioned above. Some suggestions follow which might enable this.

Pretend play
Materials and equipment which allow children to act out scenes from daily life by dressing up and by pretending to be adults or peers in roleplay.

Messy play
This involves activities with real clay, finger-painting, cake and bread making, and so on. Children's reactions to messiness can be revealing.

'Smelly' toys and objects
These can include foam-rubber dolls and figures, plasticine and other materials. Smells can prompt the recall of memories. Smelly objects and textured ones such as stickle bricks, rough and felt-like surfaces could provide a focus for the fascination with textures which can be seen in some childhood disorders.

Life-like toys
Most toys allow for children to reveal thoughts and emotions, but some are more likely than others to encourage such responses. Life-like dolls can be used by children to tell about fears and anxieties caused by some situations. Conversing through a doll as if it were a member of the group can protect a child from an adult's question and answer sessions which can feel very direct and threatening to children.

Colouring and drawing materials
These allow children to express themselves indirectly. They also reveal their motor skills. Children sometimes find it easier to indicate in colours and drawings any thoughts and feelings which they have not the words to express.

Noise-producing objects
For example, musical instruments, speaking dolls and tape players are useful. Reactions to sound can provide diagnostic information: hearing impairment, specific language disorder, sensory reactions in brain damage and autism, and so on.

Collections of objects
These could be buttons, bottle tops, marbles, etc. They can be used for colour and other labelling activities, for sorting into groups and matching exercises. Jigsaws and construction toys rely upon visuo-spatial skills (using vision to organize objects into a pattern) and visuo-motor skills (coordinating eyes and limbs to assemble something). These activities can bring to light perceptual and problem-solving difficulties found in brain damage, in mental and physical handicap and in more general problems concerned with the development of children's language and thinking.

When working with children in playrooms equipped appropriately, vigilant carers should notice any signs of physical, mental, emotional and social disorder. As a basis for deciding whether to seek the help of other professionals, use the seven pointers in the general guidelines earlier in this chapter (pages 85–6).

Key questions

Use these questions to check back over the material covered in this chapter and assess your grasp of it, before moving on. Discuss the questions, and responses to them, with colleagues and tutors.

- What do you have to take into account before deciding that the behaviours a child is showing are a cause for professional concern?
- How might the facilities in a play area help to reveal a child's need for special professional attention?

Relevant S/NVQ Units

The material in this chapter will help with preparation for the following Child Care and Education S/NVQ Units: C4, C5, C6, C7, C9, C10 and C11.

Further reading

Douglas, Jo (1989) *Behaviour Problems in Young Children*, London: Routledge. Chapter 9 'The overactive and hyperactive child'.

Richman, N. and Lansdown, R. (1988) *Problems of Pre-school Children*, Chichester: John Wiley. Chapter 5 'Language and communication'; table 5.3 on page 68 gives useful guidelines about when to refer.

Webb, N. B. (1991) *Play Therapy with Children in Crisis*, New York: Guilford Press. A case-book detailing various techniques for use with children who have suffered crises resulting from a parent's death, fostering, violence, medical intervention and natural disasters.

Activity

Selecting play activities for diagnostic purposes

The purpose of this activity is to develop awareness of the diagnostic potential of playroom equipment.

Organization

This activity is suitable for completion by individuals or by small groups of five or fewer. Groups should choose someone to serve as group leader and to record the group's discussion.

1. Refer to the information given in Chapter 10 under the heading 'A play environment for diagnostic purposes' and create an inventory sheet for grouping toys and equipment into categories which will indicate their purpose in a playroom.
2. Individually, list the range of toys and equipment in your own place of work or work placement agency.
3. Group members should give the list to the group leader. The group leader should read out the items on each list.
4. The individual or the group should decide which item fits into each category. Each person should enter the item in that category on their inventory sheet. Leaders should return the group members' lists.
5. Individuals or groups should consider the content of each category and decide whether the playroom needs any additional toys or equipment useful for uncovering activities and attitudes among children, for diagnostic purposes.
6. Each group member should compare the item inventory of the group with her or his own.

Activity

Using play as a diagnostic tool

Organization
This activity is suitable for completion by individuals or by small groups of five or fewer. Groups should choose someone to serve as group leader and to record the group's discussion.

1 Choose from Chapter 10 one area of special need; study it and discuss it.
   (a) Individuals: on a piece of paper, list the most important indicators of this special need.
   (b) Groups: each group member in turn should mention one important characteristic which children with that special need might show in a play situation. Continue this until the group has mentioned all the most important indicators of this special need.
2 Write these characteristics on a piece of paper or display them on a blackboard, overhead projector or large sheet of paper.
3 Consider in what circumstances during play a child might reveal each characteristic or diagnostic sign. Write this alongside each characteristic displayed.
4 Those who are in a special-needs placement or who have a child with special needs in their own place of work should either use this table to create an inventory for observing the child or devise their own observation chart for recording the important behaviours of a child with a different need.
5 If time permits, repeat this exercise with a different type of special need. Compare the two sets of diagnostic signs and the play circumstances in which they might be noticed.

11

Partnership with parents

Preview

This chapter considers:

- the importance of partnership between caring agencies and families;
- the legislative context of partnership;
- parental rights and duties;
- what constitutes good parenting;
- what is involved in partnership;
- barriers to partnership;
- what constitutes good practice in partnership.

Partnership between caring agencies and families

The policies and procedures of many agencies create powerful barriers to partnership. Tensions in creating partnerships are often reflected in working practices which conflict with providing any parental involvement. The idea that there should be partnership between workers and parents goes back about 20 years. It can be linked to a mounting awareness of the public's need to have a voice in local government and in the delivery of services to individuals, families and communities particularly in the areas of education, health and welfare.

More and more people working in professional education and in the care of children need to work within a network of family, informal carers and other professionals. They also need to take into consideration that the family exists within a multi-cultural context and that the stresses of poverty, poor housing, unemployment, racism and sexism can affect the way a family functions.

Professional carers are involved in helping families to care for their own children and they also have a part to play in protecting those children. They have the core task of creating and developing partnerships with parents. This has important implications for professional practice in the following ways:

- day-to-day communication;
- talking to parents about what their child did during the day develops a close working relationship;
- mentioning any concerns you have or problems the child may have maintains open communication.

The legislative context of partnership

The Children Act 1989 in England and Wales and the Children (Northern Ireland) Order 1993 reaffirm the view that the Government believes that children are best looked after within their families. It gives voluntary and statutory agencies the responsibility for working in partnership with parents, and stresses that the best way to promote child care and help with child raising is for professionals to develop a good working partnership with parents.

To this end, both the Act and the Order use the phrase 'parental responsibility' to sum up the collection of duties, rights and authority which a parent has towards a child. They emphasize that:

- children should not be viewed as the property of parents;
- child rearing is primarily the responsibility of parents;
- the role of the state is to assist parents with these responsibilities but not to interfere in family life.

In this context, the status of parent extends to others involved in the care and upbringing of children; thus extended family members, grandparents, step-parents, child-minders or foster parents and unmarried fathers may be considered as sharing parental responsibility.

> The important thing is that natural parents cannot surrender their parental responsibility.

The all-embracing concept of parental responsibility includes the following parental rights and duties:

Parental rights
These include the right:

1 to determine where the child should live;
2 to determine education;
3 to determine religion;
4 to discipline the child;
5 to authorize medical treatment;
6 to appoint a guardian;
7 agree to adoption;
8 consent to the child's marriage;
9 to consent to change in the child's name;
10 to administer the child's property.

Parental duties
These include the duty:

1 to protect the child;
2 to control the child;
3 to provide financial support for the child;
4 to ensure the child's education.

The duties of the local authority

These include the duty:

- to find out about children in need in their area;
- to provide a range of services and resources to support families of children in need;
- to provide both parents and children with information about what services are available;
- to develop procedures for seeking children's and parents' views about the service they receive.

What is involved in parenting?

The first question to ask about parenting is whether those responsible for caring for children are meeting their needs. These needs include physical safety and care, love and praise, security, stimulation, and developing a child's self-identity (see Chapter 2).

> Research shows that problems are caused when carers are able to satisfy some needs but not others.

Child-abuse inquiries demonstrate how difficult it is to assess parent–child relationships which are not consistently bad, but vary in quality. Such relationships depend upon other factors, such as low income, poverty, poor housing, poor health and the carer's capacity to cope with such stress. Poverty is a crucial factor in the backgrounds of family difficulties and often leads to children being removed into care. Adults' own experiences as children, as well as the quality of their current social relationships, significantly affect their capacity to look after children.

There is a larger number of mixed racial children in public care than might be expected from the number in the population as a whole. The significance of racial and ethnic issues relating to parenting emphasizes the need to examine cultural differences in family relationships. Fahlberg (1979) proposed that parenting could be considered from three perspectives:

- birth parent;
- legal parent;
- parenting parent.

Birth parent

The birth parent is responsible for life itself, the sex, physical looks, intellectual potential and predisposition for certain diseases.

Legal parent

The legal parent is responsible for making decisions about things like schooling, where the child lives, health and safety issues and financial security.

Parenting parent
The parenting parent is responsible for providing love, stimulation, discipline, food, clothes and toys, and care when the child is unwell.

This classification is useful because it enables us to see that parenting can be a shared activity with more than one person involved with children. In families, these responsibilities can be shared or delegated to others.

But what is 'unsatisfactory parental care'?

This question lies at the heart of many decisions about child protection. The Social Services Inspectorate issued guidance about aspects of parenting which may be harmful for children, but there is less official guidance about where to draw the line between what is acceptable or unacceptable parenting. Much research has focused on trying to identify how parents can behave in the best possible way to promote their children's development and best interests.

Pugh and De Ath (1989), for example, try to answer the question: 'How can parents best fulfil their parenting tasks?' There are four areas where parents may require support and guidance from statutory agencies:

- creating opportunities for children;
- information about child development;
- coping with children;
- understanding themselves.

Creating opportunities for children
Parents who are already disadvantaged by life experiences cannot meet their children's needs. They may need the experience of being parented themselves before they can respond to their own children. You may know of some parents who seem to be competing for attention alongside their children and appear to be more needy than their offspring. Such parents may have had very poor experiences as children. By helping to take account of the parents' personal needs, the professional carer is indirectly caring for the children.

Information about child development
Parents need information and knowledge about child development and what can be expected at different ages and stages. Magazines go some way to meeting this need but families on low incomes may be unable to afford these and may find them difficult to read. Families also need information about benefits entitlement and health and education issues.

Coping with children
Parenting skills also include budgeting, running a home, home maintenance such as changing plugs, painting and decorating, and providing a good diet for family members. The core skills demanded are more like those of a 'superparent', such as coping with stress and dealing with conflict, being consistent in attitudes and behaviour, being able to respond to changing needs and demands.

Understanding themselves
Finally, they need to understand themselves as people and as parents and how their

attitudes and values affect their parenting. Caring for children is a demanding task which requires maturity, insight, self-awareness, patience, and a willingness continually to place children's needs first. Realistically, most parents cannot meet these demands but provide good enough parenting with help from family and friends. It is not clear how far most care centres and schools take account of these needs. Writers and researchers tend to single out female carers, raising the question of why men are not automatically included in all discussions about parenting.

What is involved in partnership?

Since the 1960s there has been a movement among professional carers towards involving parents as partners in the care and education of children, rather than just taking over, as tended to happen previously. The Plowden Report (1967) highlighted how parental attitudes towards their children's education vitally influenced their school performance. The recommendations of most of the major education reports over the past 25 years have not influenced practice despite an acceptance in theory of the need for closer relationships with parents. An indication of this has been how few reports prior to the 1980s focused on the concept of partnership.

Partnership in pre-school caring

One of the most influential studies undertaken was by Pugh and De Ath in the 1980s. This explored how far services for children under five were planned, implemented and delivered in partnership with parents. They recommended several initiatives where such a working partnership had been achieved – in health education, the social services and the voluntary sector.

Pugh and De Ath developed a framework of five categories to help workers with children under five to evaluate their work with parents.

Categories of parental involvement

Non-participation

This refers to parents who use a pre-school service but do not involve themselves in how it operates. There are two kinds of non-participation:

- active non-participation – parents are unable to participate because they are working or are using the respite care services;
- passive non-participation – parents would like to be involved but lack either the confidence or energy to participate, or cannot because English is not their first language.

Support

This refers to parents who offer support by fundraising, promoting the centre's philosophy, attending specific functions such as coffee mornings, fashion shows and annual general meetings. They reinforce the centre's activities at home, for example by singing nursery rhymes and playing with playdough or water.

Participation

This involves parents working together with staff, either through going on outings with children, being involved in working a rota or toy library or participating in training sessions.

Partnership

A working relationship exists with shared sense of purpose, respect and willingness to negotiate. Partnership also implies that parents and workers share information, responsibility, skills, decision making and accountability. This is evident in a number of ways.

- Partnership between individual parents as co-workers, carers or educators and professionals:
  - with equal access to information and records;
  - sharing in decision-making for their child;
  - sharing in development of care plans and reviews and monitoring of their child.
- Partnership between parents in general and a particular centre. This involves participation in:
  - planning and management;
  - formulation of aims and objectives;
  - staff selection;
  - selection of children;
  - evaluation of the centre's work.
- Partnership between parents as workers and a centre, for example:
  - visiting other parents at home;
  - running groups;
  - counselling other parents;
  - becoming child-minders and playgroup leaders.
- Partnership between parents and policy-makers in the community:
  - membership of under-fives liaison group;
  - Pre-school Playgroup Association's regional committee;
  - liaison with local education, health and social services committees.

Control

Parents are ultimately responsible and accountable for the control of the centre or for specific aspects, such as management of budget and resources, formulating aims and objectives and deciding how the centre will be run.

This framework is a useful device for analysing how user friendly a particular centre is, whether partnership is encouraged or discouraged or where the balance of power lies in relationships between workers and parents. Which activities they feel parents should be involved in varies from centre to centre. For example, they may encourage parents to be involved in their own children's play but not wish to encourage them to take part in the group as a whole or, for health and safety reasons, to set up a tea/coffee rota. In other centres, parents may be represented on management committees.

Thus some agencies involved in providing pre-school facilities may pay only lip-service to the importance of involving parents and fail to recognize or take account of the negative effect professionals can have on parents.

Pugh and De Ath's work on partnership was further developed by Barnardos in a research project with the University of Bristol in 1987–1988. 'Aiming for Partnership' by Daines, Lyon and Parsloe (Barnardos, 1990) looked at the realities of establishing partnerships in services for children and families. They believed true partnership contained three elements:

- mutual support;
- ability to work together sharing care;
- mutual control power sharing over the service especially in decision-making.

They studied four projects and found that most encouraged a high degree of parental participation but were not operating genuine partnership. They devised a classification for parental participation which was very similar to Pugh and De Ath's framework. There were three levels of participation:

1 personal;
2 organizational;
3 local/national.

Examples of personal participation are:

- planning, implementing and reviewing care programmes for parents and children;
- contributing to the day-to-day running of the centre;
- promoting the centre and representation on committees;
- contributing to research data and representation at local and national level.

The study concluded that partnership was essential, but that it could not be achieved. Instead they advocated 'maximum feasible participation' which encouraged as much choice as possible in partnership. Thus partnership is an ever-changing process which evolves through developing practices and policies but is rarely achieved as a goal.

Ironically, the emphasis on partnership in the emergence of recent child-care legislation and principles would lead one to think the difficulties involved in implementing genuine partnership could be resolved by statute. This is a far cry from the realities and tensions which exist.

Barriers to partnership

The most obvious barrier to partnership is the power imbalance which exists between families, parents, children and professional carers.

At its most basic level, staff engaged in the professional care of children have access to training. In some facilities, other agencies refer children and families. This creates potential barriers as families may feel threatened by the professionals' use of language and unfamiliar ways of work. The emphasis on the welfare of children has often meant that parents' needs and wishes have to take a back seat as agencies concentrate their professional focus on the children.

Pugh and De Ath's study highlights three main areas where barriers occur:

- the centre itself;
- the skills and attitudes of staff;
- the motivation and level of parents' confidence

The centre itself

- What is the overall aim of the agency? Is it a community-based, self-help project or is it offering specialist help to families where parenting skills are a cause for concern?
- Does it have a policy statement on working with parents? Are there practice guidelines on the implementation of the policy and have staff received training for this? What role do parents play and is this included in the aims of the centre? To what extent are there clear expectations that parents will be involved?
- Is the role of the management committee clear? Where does the power lie for decision-making? What decisions can this committee make? What procedures are there for access to records? Have workers identified and discussed issues related to confidentiality? Have workers offered parents any involvement in management? How 'user friendly' are meetings?
- Is the centre adequately funded? What are the sources of financial assistance? What is the level of staffing? To what extent is the centre able to raise its own funds?
- How accessible and welcoming are the premises? What publicity information is available and in what languages?

Skills and attitudes of staff

- Do centre staff listen and understand difficulties from a family point of view?
- Is there an ethos which is supportive of staff and the development of partnership?
- To what extent are parents involved as evaluators of the services? Is feedback actively sought and by what methods?
- How do staff try to meet parents' needs? Do staff have a shared sense of purpose, mutual respect and willingness to negotiate?

Parents' level of confidence

- Do parents feel valued as partners in their own right with valuable skills to offer?
- To what extent are parents empowered to be involved in working with children?
- Can parents identify benefits to themselves and their children?
- What are parental perceptions of staff involvement?
- Are parents involved in written agreements and reviews?

The term 'parents', although used in the plural, implies that both mothers and fathers are involved. Most research does not distinguish between the effects of maternal and paternal participation upon children development. (Refer to Chapter 1 of this book for more details.) Research also focuses on the role of women both as recipients and as providers of such services and the difficulties posed by beliefs held of gender, race and class. For example, workers may hold stereotypical assumptions of male involvement in nurturing (men may be viewed as the head of the household, and the main decision-makers). Alternatively, workers may support the idea of house husbands.

So, what is the challenge of anti-sexist practice? In simple terms it is the attempt:

- to achieve empowerment for women;
- to focus on parents not simply mothers;
- to address the pressure inherent in the caring role;
- to guard against enforcing dependency in women who use such services.

The difficulty of this task cannot be overestimated against a backcloth of a low-status, undervalued, female work group who are largely responsible for the face-to-face delivery of services to children and parents.

Key questions

Use these questions to check back over the material covered in this chapter and assess your grasp of it, before moving on. Discuss the questions, and responses to them, with colleagues and tutors.

- How has the idea of partnership developed?
- What is involved in parenting?
- What are the components of partnership?
- What are the barriers to achieving partnership between workers and parents?

Relevant S/NVQ Units

The material in this chapter will help with preparation for the following Child Care and Education S/NVQ Units: P2, P3 and P5.

Further reading

Wolfendale, S. (ed.) (1989) *Parental Involvement: Developing Networks between School, Home and Community*, London: Cassell. Chapter 1 is a good starting point for 'partnership'.

Daines, R., Lyon, K. and Parsloe, P. (1990) *Aiming for Partnership*, Essex: Barnardos Practice Paper. This is an account of research undertaken in four Barnardos projects which encouraged parental participation. Some parts are academic but the accounts of particular projects make easy reading.

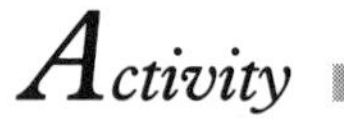

Involving parents in care work

This activity – and each of those following this one – is designed to enable workers to appraise their own working environments and working practices.

Organization

This activity may be completed as a member of a group.

1 Compile a list of your centre's activities with children.
2 Identify current ways in which parents are involved in your agency, paying attention to the framework developed by Pugh and De Ath.
3 Comparing the list of activities and the ways in which parents are involved, identify where you feel the gaps lie.
4 Pooling the group's feedback on this exercise draw up two lists of:

(a) ways in which parents are involved in facilities for the under-fives;
(b) current difficulties in achieving partnership as identified from individual exercises.

5 As a group, discuss ways in which parental involvement could be improved and consider how these would realistically be applied to your own work setting.

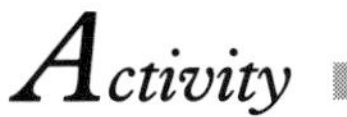

Negotiating parental involvement in care work

Organization
This activity is suitable for individuals.

1 Identify a parent whose child attends your centre and with whom you wish to work out an agreement about their involvement.
2 Record your initial feelings about approaching the parent.
3 Plan in advance how you will explain the nature of your exercise, what questions you will ask and how you will record the information.
4 Arrange a meeting with the parent and negotiate an agreement, keeping records of what was agreed.
5 After completing the agreement, record your experience noting any difficulties and reasons for these.
6 List several points of learning achieved.

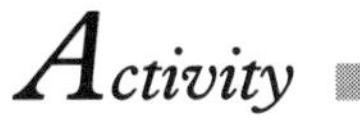

Promoting parental responsibility

Organization
This activity may be completed by an individual or undertaken as a member of a group.

1 Consider or discuss your understanding of 'parental responsibility' and reflect on the implications this has for your work setting.
2 Identify ways in which your facility assists with parental responsibility.

Activity

Introducing parenting skills

Preparation: a briefing on roleplays
This activity uses roleplay: a very popular training technique which involves the spontaneous acting out of a situation by selected members of a group. It encourages active participation and offers insights into the feelings and attitudes of others. It also develops an understanding of the realms of emotions experienced in a particular situation. Roleplay is a powerful medium for allowing people to explore problems or issues and great care must be taken in the essential stages of briefing, enacting, debriefing and deroling.

- **Briefing** – establish the scenario and determine the roles to be played.
- **Enacting** – allocate the roles to individuals, while being sensitive to the characteristics of the group. Establish ground rules for interaction, for example:
  1 Respect other people's feelings enough to listen when they are expressing them.
  2 Recognize that other people have different experiences which lead them to think and feel differently.
  3 Remember that roleplays involve an element of acting and respect other roleplayers; do not act aggressively or in a way which may cause offence or distress. Brief the participants about their roles and act out the scene.
- **Debriefing** – allow plenty of time for the discussion and analysis of both the *content* of the interaction – what people said and did – as well as the *process* – how they said or did it.

- **Deroling** – individuals can become very emotionally involved in the role they are playing and it is important that they are given the opportunity to calm any strong feelings and to return to their own role when the exercise is finished. Encourage participants to make a statement to the group, such as 'I am . . . and I work as a carer in . . .'. Allow time for participants to discuss how they felt while enacting the roleplay and what they have learnt from the activity.

Organization
This activity can be undertaken as a member of a group.

1 Discuss how your centre approaches parenting skills with parents who attend.
2 Undertake a roleplay exercise with three participants – one person playing a parent, another a member of staff, the third an observer.
3 Select an incident from your personal experience where you had to discuss parenting skills with a parent. This will form the basis of the roleplay.
4 Each participant should think about their feelings prior to the roleplay and record them.
5 Undertake a 10–15 minute roleplay focusing on introducing the subject of parenting skills and discussing this with the parent.
6 Share your observations of the roleplay only with the participants. Observers should concentrate on giving factual information about their observations avoiding opinions and judgements; for example, in your introduction you did not explain why the meeting was taking place/the parent did not have eye contact with the worker. (See Chapter 9 for further details.) Your observations should note the following:
(a) How does the worker introduce the subject of parenting skills?
(b) How does the parent react?
(c) What is the outcome?
7 Each participant should discuss the observer's feedback. Focus on what it felt like to be in the role of worker and parent. As worker, was it easy or difficult to discuss an aspect of parenting skill? Was appropriate language used? Was jargon avoided? As parent, how did you feel when the worker raised the subject? Did you experience emotions of defensiveness, anger, annoyance or feel you were being helped to discuss the matter? How did the worker do this?
8 Record your learning about the helpful ways to introduce discussion of parenting skills with parents.

12

Team membership and teamwork

Preview

This chapter looks at:

- why teams are important;
- defining teams and teamwork;
- stages in the life of a team;
- how the style of team leadership adopted affects team members' morale and actions;
- ways of contributing to your team.

Why are teams important?

A significant proportion of our working lives is spent interacting with others, often in groups. People in groups influence each other in many ways. Any group is formed from a complex interaction of roles, expectations, individual personalities and hidden agendas. Group pressures can exert a major influence over the behaviour of individual members. Carers need to have some understanding of the sort of team they work in, what stage of development the team has achieved and the leadership style which operates. They derive support and guidance from their teams. Staff morale is affected by relationships within the team and the leadership given to staff members.

Although the majority of workers in child care and education work within a group, not all groups can be called teams because they may not have all the distinguishing features of a team.

Defining teams and teamwork

Some writers have distinguished between the idea of a team, and a network. Hey (1979) thought the team involved regular interaction between a small group of people working together permanently and for a long period of time. A network was defined by Hey as working with a wide range of people, often engaged in shift work, and rarely all working simultaneously.

Another important feature of teamwork, according to Payne and Scott (1982), is its instrumental and expressive aspects. (See Chapter 3 for discussion of these aspects.)

Instrumental activities are concerned with:

- getting the work done;
- allocating and planning agreed work;
- getting the best out of people by matching knowledge and skills;
- looking at how you have worked.

The term 'expressive activities' relates to the extent to which the team members:

- motivate each other;
- offer support in times of stress;
- are open about receiving feedback about their work.

Feedback is the information you give other people about how you feel towards them and what you want from them. The importance of feedback, whether positive or negative, is that it gives you a clearer picture of how people see you. It enables you to understand the effect you have on others and consequently to change behaviours if you want to.

Ultimately, personal contributions to a group depend on how people feel about the team; whether there is an trusting, open, friendly environment in which to work or whether there is an uncomfortable atmosphere with constant griping, and backstabbing and concerns over watching your back.

Most writers agree that teams have:

- an awareness of group identity;
- a common aim;
- agreed values and norms which set standards of practice.

Thus staff who work together in a playgroup could be considered a team because they share a responsibility:

- to promote the playgroup as a service for children and families in the local community (awareness of group identity);
- to care for children (common aim);
- to provide play and stimulation (agreed values and norms);
- to maintain health and safety (agreed values and norms).

A norm is a term which refers to behaviours which people are expected to adhere to. When people deviate from agreed norms they are usually put under pressure from others to conform. Norms can be established about such things as acceptable dress, punctuality or how group members will interact, for example, taking turns in discussion and not interrupting. Most teams start as work groups and as each member makes a contribution towards the agreed purpose of the group, collaboration develops and members come to depend on each other's contributions.

Stages in the life of a team

Teams rarely come into existence fully formed. Tuckman (1965) put forward the idea that a group grows, matures and develops like a living organism and moves through a cycle of four stages of development:

- forming;
- storming;
- norming;
- performing.

It has been suggested that teams also go through similar stages of development.

Forming stage
At this stage the members do not know each other and it is a period of discovering and understanding others' attitudes and backgrounds. The key feature here is the need for introductions, using exercises to break the ice and to look at the needs and expectations of individual members. The leader has an important role to play in ensuring contributions from all participants. At this stage, first impressions are very important.

Storming stage
This is the conflict stage with disagreements over the purpose of the group, challenges to the leader, and personality clashes between particular members. This can feel a very uncomfortable stage of a group formation but it is healthy because it allows for openness and challenge. If groups do not work through this, conflicts may emerge at a later stage.

Norming stage
Here the group agrees a way of working together. Members may make an explicit agreement about some things, for instance, how to handle issues over confidentiality, but other things may be implicit, for instance, whether members will take it in turns to operate a coffee rota. Members sort out working rules and norms and allocate roles. For example, a line manager outside the group may expect the team leader to hold staff meetings, decide work rotas and negotiate with outside agencies.

Performing stage
This is the stage when the group is working well together and trust has been built up. Group members are usually very positive and full of energy, enthusiastic about their work. The team has developed good working relationships, support is evident and there is a good atmosphere.

Tuckman points out three particular problems that may arise for groups working together:

- effective group functioning may be hindered because members have differing perspectives and are not explicit about this;
- the purpose of the group may not be clarified, so confusing group members about their role;
- groups need to progress through each stage before they can work properly together.

The importance of leadership style

Leadership style has received a lot of attention because research has shown that style influences the behaviour, beliefs and attitudes of those who work together in teams.

Research has also demonstrated that we conform to others' views to varying degrees and under certain circumstances. Such influence is not one sided and in turn, we play an important role in influencing and controlling others. Leadership style is also influential in promoting job satisfaction and some writers have linked job stress to lack of supportive leadership. Three differing leadership styles can be distinguished:

- autocratic leadership,
- laissez-faire leadership,
- democratic leadership.

Autocratic leadership

The autocratic style of leader involves displaying little confidence or trust in workers. Decisions are imposed without consultation or involvement from other workers in the team. There is little communication or opportunity to influence any decisions which may be taken. On the whole, workers in the team feel they are given instructions about how to work and are not encouraged to be critical or to change their ways of working.

Laissez-faire leadership

The laissez-faire style of leader allows the team to make their own decisions, but is available to help if needed. The team itself is responsible for the day-to-day work, as well as budgeting and evaluating how well the work is being carried out. This style of leadership can place strain on workers who may feel a lack of direction, guidance or support.

Democratic leadership

The democratic style of leadership is one where the team has a greater say in the development of policies, procedures, methods of working and recruitment of staff. Individual talents and contributions are valued and acknowledged. Workers feel motivated and willing to share ideas and opinions. Mutual respect is evident and workers in the team appear to have a vested interest in how the team operates.

How to make the best contribution to your team

It is important to acknowledge that individual members bring their own strengths and weaknesses and skills to the team. The worker's contribution to the team's overall effectiveness is vital, and there are a number of important characteristics workers need in order to develop their own confidence and enable them to make a better contribution to their team. These include:

- self-esteem,
- assertiveness skills,
- promoting emotional health.

Self-esteem

As we noted in Chapter 3 an adult's self-esteem is developed through childhood experience. Some adults experience feelings of low self-esteem and are lacking in confidence about their abilities and self worth.

The discussion of rational emotive therapy and self-talk techniques for children in Chapter 6 can apply to adults.

Assertiveness skills

Personal or professional relationships involve a matter of give and take between people involved in them. Being assertive means that people have control over their situation by respecting people's feelings and ensuring this is reciprocated.

The essential feature of assertiveness is being able to express personal feelings in such a way that people listen. Assertiveness enables people to own their own thoughts, and to exert their rights and particularly their feelings in the face of opposition. Skills of assertion are particularly important in an area of work where women predominate and there are issues of low status.

The following model outlines a method of using assertiveness in communication. The steps have been reproduced with permission from a model devised by M. Smyth (1994).

Step-by-step method of using assertiveness in communication

1. 'Tune in' to your own feelings about the situation. Tuning in is a means of developing an awareness of your inner feelings.
2. Put your feelings into words (by yourself).
3. Make connections between your feelings and others' behaviour; for example, 'I feel angry when you discuss my work in front of others.'
4. 'Tune in' to your listener's feelings. What might they be feeling in their position? Were they trying to be critical of your work?
5. Contract with your listener for a discussion. 'I would like to discuss with you what you have been saying about my work.'
6. Make the statement, showing how you have tuned in to their feelings. 'You were probably not happy with my work but when you discuss it in front of others, I feel angry.'
7. Listen actively to their feedback and if necessary return to step 3 connecting your own feelings with others' behaviour as you discuss the situation.

Promoting emotional health

Knowledge of how body and mind react to the demands placed on people is crucial in the area of working with children. This work often results in stress and there are a number of potential sources of stress or stressors in the workplace. Some of these are desirable and necessary to ensure work is carried out. Some stressors are temporary while others are permanent.

Work-related stressors

1. Change in the workplace.
2. Poor working conditions, for example, long hours, overcrowding, little natural light or ventilation.
3. Communication difficulties between workers.
4. Role conflict, for example, family versus work demands.
5. Role overload, for example, having to fulfil too many responsibilities.

6 Role uncertainty, for example, joining a new team.
7 Stress related to working directly with children and their families.

Sometimes too much stress can lead to burnout. This has been described as a state which occurs when workers are emotionally exhausted, have little sense of job satisfaction and feel unable to face or cope with the daily demands of their job. It begins with feelings of dissatisfaction at work and leads to thinking that there is no point in sharing feelings of stress. Workers find it difficult to share their feelings with others and are afraid of making a mistake or being unable to cope.

As the symptoms increase, gradually it becomes difficult to 'switch off' from work and anxiety and panic attacks can develop. The pattern of burnout can lead on from casual sick days to eventual physical and mental breakdown.

Every individual has a personal responsibility to take care of their own emotional health and take steps to combat or reduce stress in their lives. This usually includes a combination of exercise, healthier lifestyle, time management and developing assertiveness skills.

Key questions

Use these questions to check back over the material covered in this chapter and assess your grasp of it, before moving on. Discuss the questions, and responses to them, with colleagues and tutors.

- What is the difference between a team and a network?
- How do teams affect team members and group morale?
- What are the different types of leadership style?
- How can workers make a more effective contribution to their teams?

Relevant S/NVQ Unit

The material in this chapter will help with preparation for the following Child Care and Education S/NVQ Unit: M4.

Further reading

Mullins, L. J. (1985) *Management and Organizational Behaviour*, London: Pitman. Parts 7 and 8 are useful on the nature of groups and leadership.

Payne, M. (1982) *Working in Teams*, London and Basingstoke: The Macmillan Press Ltd. Written primarily as a guide to teamwork in helping services, it is easily read and digested.

Buchanan, D. A., and Huczynski, A. A. (1985) *Organizational Behaviour: An Introductory Text*, Hemel Hempstead: Prentice-Hall International. Designed for students with no background in social science. Clearly laid out and is the sort of text that could be dipped into.

Activity

Personal relationships within a team

This activity enables the worker to look at how people in groups influence each other.

1. Individually reflect on your team or workplace, its leadership style, gender, and age composition. Include details of how long members have been appointed to their particular posts and what their roles and responsibilities involve. Do not forget to include yourself.
2. Compile a separate list of staff members and map out who relates to whom. You could use broken lines to indicate little contact between individuals and an unbroken line to suggest close relationships.
3. Draw up a list of staff members and their roles and responsibilities. Note any overlap which occurs or any specialist skills which members possess.
4. Record your learning about relationships in the team and overlap in team roles and responsibilities.

Activity

Working as a member of a team

This activity will promote a worker's self-awareness and self-worth through evaluation of personal strengths.

1. Individually compile a lifeline chart. A lifeline can be drawn in many ways. It can be a simple way of reviewing your own life by recording and reflecting on the things that stand out. Draw a line like a snake and insert key events in your life. Select those experiences which have been important to you, for example, marriage, bereavement, birth of a child, friendships, moving house, taking a new job or new responsibilities.
2. Choose one of those events and write out a description of why it has been important to you and how it has influenced you in future events.
3. Write down the skills and abilities you were using at the time, for example:
   - communicating – making telephone calls, writing letters, making appointments;
   - dealing with people – being able to listen to others, offering advice, keeping calm in the face of crisis.
4. List three skills and three personal qualities you possess.
5. In pairs, share your list with another person, prefacing each skills with 'I am good at . . .' and qualities with 'I know I am a good . . . '.
6. Afterwards, discuss the exercise with your partner reflecting on ways to build up self-esteem.

Activity

Roleplay of team scenarios

This activity illustrates how different leadership styles affect team members.

Preparation

Read chapter 12, and read the notes on roleplay on page 104.

1. Working in small groups devise a roleplay situation which would represent a team meeting. Decide who will play the team leader and agree the scenario you will enact. For example, it could be a meeting to discuss training information or the selection of a new staff member.
2. The team leader should choose a leadership style to adopt – autocratic, democratic or laissez-faire.
3. Undertake the roleplay and on completion discuss the style adopted and the effects on membership contributions. Perhaps you can repeat the roleplay but using a different leadership style.

Activity

Coping with stress

1. Contact your local health promotions officer and obtain a pack about coping with stress and healthier lifestyles.
2. Consider the content, particularly any questionnaires related to coping with stress.
3. Review your own methods of coping with stress.
4. Devise a strategy for yourself and make out a weekly diary for stress reduction.
5. Review your diary on a monthly basis.

13
Protecting children

Preview

This chapter deals with:

- historical factors which affect the protection of children such as:
  - the role of the state in family life,
  - society's attitudes towards children,
  - how child abuse emerged as a problem;
- definitions and categories of child abuse;
- theories about why abuse occurs;
- signs and symptoms of different forms of abuse;
- issues for children with special needs;
- guidelines for good practice.

Historical factors

Child abuse affects personal life and professional work. It is a sad fact that some people reading this chapter and carrying out the activities were, or have been, victims of abuse themselves, or may have knowledge of ongoing abusive situations. The personal impact of child abuse can be traumatic for the individuals involved. Working through the material in this chapter may reawaken memories or heighten the pain felt by making you aware of the damage you have suffered. Because the material in the main text is designed to allow reflection on an intellectual level, the impact may not be felt until you begin the activities. Equally, you may not feel you wish to disclose such information about yourself. Everyone in the group bears a responsibility for developing trust and support among group members.

There is no single cause for the abuse experienced by children. It occurs in all social classes and can be caused by parents, siblings, non-biological parents, substitute carers, childminders, foster parents, extended family members, friends, strangers and even teachers and professional carers. It is a sad irony that children can also be subject to abusive practices in the care of professionals who are responsible for their protection from abuse.

The protection of children is a broad term which requires an approach which looks at interaction between society, the family, social networks, the child, the professionals involved and the legislation. The protection of children is the concern of everyone and includes promoting children's wellbeing, as well as protection from neglect, physical, emotional and sexual abuse.

Historically, the movement for the protection of children has been affected by several factors:

- state intervention in family life;
- social attitudes towards childhood;
- the recognition of child abuse as an area of great controversy which requires a response from professionals.

State intervention in family life

For a long time, tension has existed between the family's right to privacy to rear their children and the view that the State must have the right to intervene and monitor the care provided. For example, the Poor Law Amendment Act 1889 was concerned with orphaned or abandoned children.

Children were regarded in law as possessions of their parents regardless of the quality of care provided. The State was unable to intervene because of the Rights of Property which regarded children as parents' property.

The Poor Law offered no protection to children until a revision of the legislation in 1889 decreed that Poor Law guardians could assume parental rights over children already in their care if they considered parents to be irresponsible.

Specific legislation enabling State intervention to remove children from their parents was not brought into force until the Prevention of Cruelty to Children Act 1904. Successive child-care legislation continued to reinforce the tensions between State and family life.

Some legislation emphasized a duty to keep families together while other laws reinforced powers to remove children from home. The 1989 Children Act was also concerned with striking a balance between the rights and responsibilities of the State, parents and children. In this legislation, removal of children from their parents' care was to be regarded as a 'last resort'.

Society's attitudes towards childhood

The idea of a period of life called childhood did not emerge until the seventeenth century and the concept was based on a belief that children needed discipline because they were innately bad. The harsh and cruel maltreatment inflicted on children in attempts to eradicate such tendencies was tantamount to severe abuse (De Mause, 1976).

Children were regarded as an important labour force during the nineteenth century because they worked in factories and textile mills. In due course, concern about their need for education and training led to a focus on their needs for care and protection. Legislation in the 1840s was aimed at improving conditions for children in employment, but it was not until 1889 that the NSPCC was instrumental in introducing the Prevention of Cruelty to and Protection of Children Act 1889.

Successive legislation through the twentieth century has reinforced the special identity of children and reinforced the right of all children to be protected from cruelty. Family structures are changing as divorce, cohabitation and remarriage are experienced by increasing numbers of families.

Views about the family have changed together with attitudes to individual family members. Within the family unit, the roles of men and women have also changed, owing in part to economic factors such as:

- changing employment patterns,
- unemployment in the last 10–15 years,
- increased employment of women working outside the home.

How child abuse came to be recognized as a problem

Some writers argue that child abuse is a socially constructed phenomenon – that is, the way that society perceives children has a strong bearing on the way that society treats children.

Among the sociologists who advocate such a view are Dingwall (1984) and Parton (1985). Rather than giving an individualized emphasis on prediction, treatment and cure, they drew attention to the social contexts of abuse such as:

- poverty;
- class;
- gender;
- race.

Parton, in particular, traces the historical emergence of child abuse and the role of the media and State in the perception and acknowledgement of the problem.

Dr John Caffey, an American paediatric radiologist, was influential in the discovery of physical abuse in the mid–1940s. From X-rays, Dr Caffey found that many infants who were suffering from subdural haematoma (collection of blood underneath the skull) were found to have fresh, healing and healed multiple fractures in the long bones of the arms and legs. There was no history of injury to account for the lesions or evidence of disease to predispose fracture. However, Dr Caffey did not attempt to define the source of the trauma or provide a firm label.

In 1961 Dr Kempe, another American paediatrician, coined the phrase the 'battered child syndrome'. The emotive label:

- brought wider medical attention to the problem;
- encouraged state intervention;
- defined physical child abuse as an illness which relied on the use of X-rays to aid diagnosis. The 'battered baby syndrome' was discovered in Britain in the mid–1960s with impetus from forensic pathologists and paediatricians; but at that stage neither legal or social welfare agencies were centrally involved.

Prior to 1968, there was minimal awareness of the problem outside the medical professions. Media coverage in the late 1960s laid the ground for future professional involvement by NSPCC and social services. The death of Maria Colwell in January 1973 ensured a focus on physical child abuse and priority attention by the Government and social services.

In the 1980s child sexual abuse was rediscovered by agencies and workers. The Cleveland Inquiry and the series of inquiry reports which have been published since 1974 are testimony to the attention which child abuse now attracts. *Beyond Blame* (Reder *et al.* 1993) summarized 35 major fatal child abuse inquiries since 1973; highlighting how children's vulnerability to abuse continues to be a problem.

Definitions of child abuse

There is no universally accepted definition of child abuse. Local authority policy and care and protection procedures are based on guidelines issued by the Department of Health. The suggested categories relate to registration on the Child Protection Register and acknowledge the existence of other definitions. It is difficult to estimate how much abuse actually occurs, as research definitions tend to rely on statistics and not all cases of child abuse come to the attention of the authorities. Chapter 10 focused on signs of abuse which were most likely to reveal themselves in play behaviours. The following categories offer a more comprehensive overview of the various forms of abuse and specific indicators.

Categories of child abuse

Neglect
A child's basic needs for food, clothing, warmth and medical care are either deliberately or inadvertently ignored. Children are left alone or unsupervised on occasions.

Physical abuse
A child is physically hurt, injured or killed. Abuse can involve hitting, shaking, biting and excessive use of restraint.

Sexual abuse
This occurs when adults exploit children for their own sexual gratification. It may involve a variety of sexual acts including oral sex, anal or vaginal intercourse, digital penetration or penetration with objects, masturbation or showing pornographic videos.

Emotional abuse
Children are exposed to constant criticism, lack of affection, and mental bullying. They experience scapegoating – that is, being singled out for criticism or harsh comments.

Failure to thrive
Sometimes children have negative relationships with their main carers – often their mothers. The mother is unable to meet the child's needs often due to low income, little or no support, poor living conditions or family problems. This will result in a failure to thrive. Though no organic cause can be found, the child is likely to be lighter and shorter than 97 per cent of its peers.

Institutional abuse
This refers to the abuse of children by carers in residential settings. It can include any or all of the former forms of abuse. In addition, children may experience harsh punishments which are part of the method of discipline; for example, being locked in their rooms and deprived of food or water for periods of time.

Organized abuse
This is a generic term which covers abuse involving a number of abusers, children

and young people and includes different forms of abuse. It involves an element of organisation either through small paedophile or pornographic rings, or large networks of individual groups or families.

Theories of the causes of child abuse

There are a number of different theories about why child abuse occurs. One view is that child abuse is like an illness in society which can be diagnosed. This explanation would imply that a cure can be found and individual abusers treated for their 'sickness'. Such explanations do not take into account the complicated nature of child abuse, nor do they look at the wider social and cultural forces, such as poverty and low income, which impinge on the problem. It is not fully understood why people abuse children but it is necessary to try to understand abusers in order to protect children.

The following explanations summarize the main theories.

Ethological theory

This involves studies based on direct observation of animals in their natural environment. Bowlby's attachment theory is an example (see Chapter 1). This theory suggests that carers who suffered abuse as children have suffered from poor attachment experiences or maternal deprivation. As a result, they lack the ability to act as good parents, hold unrealistic expectations of their children and expect them to be easy to look after. When these expectations are not met, the carers often resort to physical ill-treatment. In such circumstances, the focus of help should be on providing supportive 'mothering' experience – that is, giving the carers an opportunity to feel cared for and in return helping to improve their ability to care for their children.

Sociobiological theory

This is based on Darwin's theory of evolution which stresses that only the strongest and fittest survive. This theory proposes that under certain stressful conditions, abuse of children can be seen as consistent with the need for survival. It suggests that carers can feel threatened by children. Abuse occurs when carers feel the children are in competition with them for attention.

Psychodynamic theory

This theory is based on Freud's work. The belief is that any form of ill- treatment in early stages of development is likely to create long-term emotional problems which can only be resolved by development of insight through therapy and counselling. If help is not received, relationships later in life could be affected, including those with children. There is an increased chance of emotional and other forms of abuse.

Behaviourist and learning theory

This is based on the view that children learn about the consequences of their behaviour through reward or punishment. Child abuse is seen to result from adults' own poor learning experiences and inadequate controlling techniques. Carers are unable to control their anger or frustration. Help is available in the form of techniques which aim to replace unacceptable parenting techniques and help abusers develop methods of self control.

Family dysfunction theory

This theory focuses on how families communicate and relate to each other. It has been applied to physical and sexual abuse to explain the process by which abuse occurs and how to treat it. Help for abusers is based on working with the whole family to try and unravel poor communication patterns. The family's difficult relationships are seen as the major cause of abuse.

Sociological theory

More attention has been focused on this theory in the United States than in the United Kingdom. It offers three main explanations for abuse.

1. Child abuse results from poor parenting skills combined with social stress and lack of family and community supports.
2. Incidence of abuse is related to widespread support for use of physical punishment of children. The family is one of the most dangerous places to live, not only for children but also for women and children, because it offers opportunities for levels of private violence which would not be publicly tolerated. Violence is passively condoned by society through a lack of determined effort to eliminate it.
3. Fundamental inequalities in society – such as poverty, poor housing, dependence on state benefits – increase the stress felt by carers.

Feminist theory

This argues that society is dominated by male interests and the male point of view. Abuse of children, particularly sexual abuse, is an example of male power. Women experience pressure from men to care for their children. Help needs to concentrate on two areas:

- being more sensitive to women's position as carers and enabling them to have a more important and valued role as parent;
- raising society's awareness of male domination and devising ways to overcome this.

Children's rights

If children were given more rights akin to adults they would be able to assert themselves. They would have more redress in cases of child abuse, and incidents would lessen.

Recognising specific indicators of abuse

Some writers suggest recognition of abuse is dependent on our willingness to entertain the possibility that it exists. Children's reactions to abuse vary. The following signs and symptoms may alert you to the possibility that a child is being neglected or physically or sexually abused. There could be reasonable explanations for all of the signs and symptoms, so do not jump to conclusions. As part of a caring network to protect children, your first duty is to the child. Knowledge of the range of normal behaviour in children will help you to be aware that a child has a particular problem but there may be many possible reasons.

Children's behaviour or appearance may give rise to concern, and further investigation of the family situation may be required to determine if the child is at risk and requires protection.

Signs and symptoms of physical abuse

Physical indicators

- Bruise marks around the face, forehead and mouth caused by facial squeezing, grabbing, blows to the head, or gripping.
- Grip marks on the legs or trunk, particularly if a child has been shaken or held down.
- Unexplained bruising in places where an injury cannot be easily sustained or explained and particularly if they are recurrent.
- Handslap marks visible on cheeks, buttocks or trunk.
- Bite marks with indentation of teeth, visible welts or bald spots.
- Burns by cigarettes or other hot objects.
- Unexplained fractures such as 'greenstick' fractures caused by twisting limbs. These are normally detected by skeletal X-ray.
- Lacerations or abrasions.
- Torn frenulum (skin inside upper lip) caused when a bottle is forced into a child's mouth during feeding.
- Dipping scalds which suggest a child has been deliberately dipped in hot water. Skin splashes are more likely to be accidental, untreated injuries.

Behavioural indicators

- Carers give improbable excuses to explain injuries.
- Child appears aggressive or withdrawn.
- Child exhibits fear of returning home.
- Child is reluctant to have physical contact.
- Clothing is worn to hide part of the body.
- Frozen awareness, child is constantly watchful of adults' reactions to him- or herself.

Signs and symptoms of neglect

Physical indicators

- Constant hunger.
- Poor state of clothing and/or personal hygiene.
- Constant tiredness.
- Anxious about being left alone.
- Untreated medical problems.
- Thin appearance, emaciation, poor condition of hair and nails.
- Child fails to reach normal developmental stages but there is no underlying medical cause for this.

Behavioural indicators

- Child experiences lack of social relationships, shunned by other children.

- Compulsive stealing, begging or scavenging.
- Low self-esteem.
- Frequently absent or late.
- Child is tired or listless.

Signs and symptoms of emotional abuse

Physical indicators

- Sudden speech disorders, stammering.
- Extremes of physical, mental and emotional development, for example, vomiting, anorexia.
- Wetting and soiling.

Behavioural indicators

- Rocking, hair twisting, thumb sucking.
- Fear of new situations.
- Attention-seeking behaviour.
- Telling lies.
- Inability to have fun.
- Indiscriminately affectionate.
- Poor peer relationships.

Signs and symptoms of sexual abuse

Physical indicators

- Soreness, bruising or bleeding in genital or anal areas, or the throat.
- Torn, stained or bloody underclothes.
- Stomach pains or headaches.
- Difficulty in walking or sitting.
- Frequent urinary or thrush infections.
- Venereal disease.
- Bedwetting, sleep disturbance.
- Loss of appetite.

Behavioural indicators

- Using sexually explicit language.
- Inappropriately seductive or precocious.
- Outbursts of anger/temper tantrums.
- Acting out sexual activity with toys.
- Fear of undressing.
- Hints at sexual activity through words, play, drawing.
- Withdrawn or isolated from other children.

Abuse of children with special needs

The increasing focus on abuse, particularly sexual abuse, has led people to realize that vulnerable groups in society, such as older people and children with special needs, are open to exploitation. Abuse of children with learning disabilities may be difficult to diagnose unless there are physical signs. Problem behaviour is too often accepted as normal for people with learning disabilities, so that symptoms which may signal alarm in a child or young person are often ignored.

Such behaviour is not recognized as a consequence of abuse and no attempts are made to find out the cause. In any situation where children are abused, it is vital that adults are able not only to recognize the signs and symptoms but are willing to bear the pain involved in hearing about the abuse.

Nowhere is it more painful than in working with children with special needs who are further victimized and disadvantaged if adult protectors are unable to reach out to them to offer protection.

Good practice guidelines for protecting children from abuse

Bearing in mind that each local authority has a child protection policy and procedure document offering guidelines to be followed in cases, or suspected cases, of child abuse, the following good practice suggestions can be used to supplement such documents.

1. Be clear about the procedures to be followed in your agency for protecting children.
2. Be prepared to act even if you feel your suspicions may not be confirmed. Report your suspicions to a senior member of staff.
3. Acknowledge your own feelings. You may be concerned about what will happen to the child or family if you raise concerns.
4. Be prepared to support your concerns with facts and remember the importance of observation and recording. (See Chapter 9 for further detail.)
5. Do not feel it is your responsibility to protect children. Resist any temptation to act as a 'lone ranger'. Research shows such behaviour only compromises children and can escalate the potential for further abuse.
6. Be willing to listen to the children and move at their pace as they share details with you. (See Chapter 8 for further detail.) Resist any temptation to probe or ask leading questions. The responsibility for child-abuse investigations rests firmly with NSPCC, statutory social services and the police. It is very important to believe what the child says. Children rarely tell lies about abuse.
7. Do not offer false reassurances to the child. Faced with a situation where a child tells you about abuse which is recurring or has occurred, do not allow them to think you can keep the knowledge to yourself. The child should not be given an absolute guarantee of confidentiality, even if this is requested as a pre-condition of telling. It should be explained to the child that certain other people may need to be told to protect him or her.
8. As soon as possible, make a written note of what the child has said.
9. Remember that abusers may not like what they do and may not be able to cope with their feelings. They require help and support to prevent them harming children.

10 Be prepared to seek professional help for yourself; dealing with children who may be abused may evoke powerful feelings or emotions.

The Children Act 1989 and protecting children from harm

The Children Act 1989 was designed to offer proper safeguards for children and opportunities for parents/carers of the child to challenge any action that the courts might take. Specific legislation on child protection can be found in Part IV of the 1989 Act. Section 31(9) says that 'harm' means ill-treatment or the impairment of health or development. 'Development' means physical, intellectual, emotional, social or behavioural development; 'health' means physical or mental health; and 'ill-treatment' includes sexual abuse and forms of ill-treatment which are not physical. Similar legislation operates in Northern Ireland in the Children (Northern Ireland) Order 1993 and in Scotland.

Key questions

Use these questions to check back over the material covered in this chapter and assess your grasp of it, before moving on. Discuss the questions, and responses to them, with colleagues and tutors.

- What factors have been influential in the protection of children?
- To what extent is child abuse a modern-day problem?
- What are the main signs and symptoms of different forms of child abuse?
- What action can workers take to protect children in their care?

Relevant S/NVQ Units

The material in this chapter will help with preparation for the following Child Care and Education S/NVQ Units: C15 and E2.

Further reading

Brown, H. and Craft, A. (eds) (1989) *Thinking the Unthinkable. Papers on Sexual Abuse and People with Learning Difficulties*, London: Family Planning Association. Papers based on a conference on sexual abuse and people with learning difficulties.

Reder et al. (1993) *Beyond Blame, Child Abuse Tragedies Revisited*, London: Routledge. Summaries of 35 major inquiries into cases of fatal child abuse. Chapter 1 is a good introduction to child protection context.

Stainton-Rogers et al. (1989) *Child Abuse and Neglect. Facing the Challenge*, London: Open University/Batsford. Directed at a general audience, this is a good basic introduction to child abuse. Chapters 1, 5, 14, 23 and 24 are worth closer examination.

Department of Health (1989) *Working Together Under the Children Act, 1989*, pages 48 and 49 provide the Department's definition of abuse.

Jones, D., Pickett, J., Oates, M. and Barbour, P. (1987) *Understanding Child Abuse*, London: Macmillan. Provides a good general introduction to the subject area.

Activity

Personal reactions to abuse

This activity enables the carer to examine their personal reactions to child abuse and the implications for working practices.

Organization

This exercise can be completed in pairs.

1 Individually reflect on the categories of abuse and write down your reactions to each form of abuse. Be honest about your responses; you may feel revulsion, disgust, despair or disbelief.
2 In pairs, share your reactions with a partner and decide what feedback you will provide to the larger group.
3 Discuss the impact your personal reactions may have on your ability to protect children.

Activity

Understanding professional roles and responsibilities in child protection work

This activity is designed to enable workers to find out about the different roles of professionals involved in child protection.

Organization

This exercise can be completed as a member of a group.

1 In a large group, identify the range of professionals involved in child protection.
2 Divide into small groups related to specific roles and draw up a list of questions to ask about their role and involvement in child protection.
3 Include questions about what signs and symptoms they might see, what action they would take and what their role is in child protection and what it means to them.
4 Agree on who will contact the professional and decide how this will be done, for example, by letter, phone call, personal contact.
5 Arrange to interview the worker and obtain the information.
6 In a large group, draw up a list of roles and responsibilities.
7 Discuss where overlap occurs and differences exist
8 Record your learning from this about the multi-professional roles in child protection.

Activity

Recognizing signs and taking action

This exercise looks at the difficulties involved in recognizing signs of abuse and deciding what action to take.

Organization

This exercise can be completed as a member of a group.

1 Select small groups which will deal with a specific abuse category, for example, physical abuse/emotional abuse.
2 Discuss the signs which would cause you to be concerned about a particular child.
3 The group must decide what symptoms would necessitate either taking immediate action, or 'keeping an eye on' or monitoring the situation.
4 Feedback to the large group (you will need to select someone who will report on the group's behalf) and note any issues involved in attempting this task.
5 As a group, discuss your learning and the implications it has for your understanding of child protection.

14

Empowerment and anti-oppressive practice

Preview

This chapter considers:

- the issue of children's rights;
- differing views on children's rights;
- UN Convention on the rights of the child;
- what constitutes children's rights;
- definitions of discrimination, oppression and empowerment;
- resources for promoting empowerment and equality;
- ways of promoting empowerment and equality.

Children's rights

The confused and sometimes contradictory attitudes of society towards children's rights are evident in everyday practices within children's homes, educational settings and institutions which offer care. For example, the European Court ruling in 1993 that a childminder could use physical punishment to discipline a child in his or her care conflicted with the policy of the National Childminding Association. The Pindown policy used in children's homes in Staffordshire was regarded as being in the child's interests; but following investigation it is now considered to be abusive in the extreme. Young people in care were denied basic human rights, subjected to enforced isolation and even refused medical treatment.

In the early 1990s the tragic death of Jamie Bulger forced us to address questions about our own children's care. The most frightening aspect of Jamie's death was its perpetration by children, which forced public opinion to recognize that violence could be inflicted on children by children themselves. The moral debate which ensued about children's rights and adult responsibilities reopened the vexed question of whether child criminals should be punished and in what way. The way in which society views the question of rights for children has varied according to the status of children and the ways in which adults in power perceive their value.

The basic definition of a right is that it is a claim to treatment which can be made by reason of law or code of practice. Denying children rights on the basis of their age and dependency may be a way for adults to perpetuate that dependency. In many respects children's rights are essentially about the power relationships between children and adults.

Differing views on children's rights

There are a number of writers who emphasize the importance of the child's own viewpoint and wishes, and view the child as a separate entity with rights to responsibility and freedom of choice. This is known as a liberationist perspective because it emphasizes that children should be treated in the same way as adults and should have access to all the rights enjoyed by adults, regardless of age.

> The child is seen as a separate entity in their own right, who should have a status more akin to that of adults.

An extreme view of children's rights

Holt (1974) wrote about children's lack of place in modern society, how this was essentially bad for them and how it could be changed. He argued that:

- Children should have access to the same rights, privileges, duties and responsibilities as adults, including the rights to vote, work, be financially independent, receive state income, lead their own lives, drive and control their learning and sexual activity.
- There should be no lower age limit for these rights and children should be able to pick and choose.
- By and large the family reinforces a child's dependency and vulnerability.
- Adults fail to recognize their children's capacities and the parent–child relationship is one of exploitation.
- Children's needs are similar to adult needs.
- Childhood is a separate world created by adults to ensure children's dependency. It is not justifiable to exclude children from their rights because they are too young.
- Holt also defended a child's right to choose a guardian. Children in America and the United Kingdom in the early 1990s who requested and were granted a divorce from their birth parents would fit into Holt's perspective.

A moderate view of children's rights

One more moderate view has been explored by Freeman (1983) who took the view that legal status should depend on a child's age. Whenever feasible children should be given a say in decision-making and policy-makers should take account of their interests.

Children's rights could be divided into:

- welfare rights and human rights;
- child protection;
- social justice;
- choice and autonomy.

Welfare rights and human rights
These include a child's right to housing, education, medical treatment, adequate nutrition and love, care and protection.

Child protection
Children are vulnerable and parents and adults have a responsibility to protect them. This applies to protection from inadequate care, abuse and neglect by carers, exploitation by employers or other forms of environmental danger, such as pollution.

Social justice
Children should have a bill of rights which makes clear statements about their rights as citizens.

Choice and autonomy
Children can choose who they live with, or can be able to challenge major parental decisions. Freeman talks about 'liberal paternalism' – adults have to protect and intervene in children's lives in order to help them develop their full maturity, but in a way that will develop their capacities to make decisions and become responsible for themselves.

Another moderate view

Archard (1993) introduces another rights perspective which he calls 'modest collectivism'. He argues that society should aim to achieve the following goals:

- collective responsibility for child care;
- diffusion of parenting;
- collective valuation of children;
- extension of children's rights.

Collective responsibility for child care
Pre-school facilities should be available for all children. Every child should be given a place at a nursery or playgroup. Such facilities should be adequately staffed by qualified staff, fulfil a clear teaching function and operate with full parental involvement.

Diffusion of parenting
Different forms of child rearing should be encouraged and parenting made available from extended family members or local communities. In this way, any adult would be able to act in a parental role towards any child – disciplining a child not their own, or dealing with a distressed child.

Collective valuation of children
Children should be seen as a valuable asset and society has a responsibility to ensure that they receive the best possible upbringing. To this end, a formal recognition of children's rights would be enshrined in a charter of children's rights and perhaps a ministerial appointment. Thus adults' ways of relating to children would be subject to scrutiny and discriminatory practices could be challenged.

Extension of children's rights
This would involve lowering the age limit for voting and exercising sexual choice. In this way, empowered by a sense of their own independence, children would be more capable of resisting exploitation by adults. Children who feel valued and cared for by society are less likely to be subjected to abuse.

The UN Convention on the Rights of the Child

The UN Convention on the Rights of the Child was an international agreement to protect children's rights. For the first time all the rights of children were written down in one document which was adopted by the UN General Assembly in 1989 and came into force in September 1990. In agreeing to the Convention, governments made a commitment to implement all the rights it contains. The UK Government agreed to be bound by the Convention in 1991. This has meant that the Government has had to make sure that our laws and the way we treat children meet the standards laid down in the Convention.

What does it contain?

The Convention sets out in a number of statements (called articles) the rights which all children and young people up to the age of 18 should have. It states children have three main rights which must be considered whenever any decision is being made about them or any action which affects them.

1 Non-discrimination – all children have equal rights whatever their race, sex, religion, language, disability, opinion or family background (Article 2).
2 Best interests – priority must be given to what would be best for the children in any decision making (Article 3).
3 The child's view – children have the right to say what they think about anything which affects them. Courts and other official bodies must listen to what children want and feel (Article 12).

Children also have civil and political rights including:

- name and nationality at birth;
- freedom of expression;
- freedom of thought, conscience and religion;
- meeting other people;
- privacy;
- access to information;
- protection from violence and harmful treatment;
- legal representation if they break the law and treatment in a way suited to their age.

The Convention also deals with economic, social, cultural and protective rights which cover the child's rights to proper standards of physical care, education, health, leisure, protection from exploitation.

The Government will report to the UN Committee on the Rights of the Child on a five-yearly basis. They will outline how they are putting the convention into practice and how they have made the public aware of the standards set out in the Convention.

Definitions of oppression and discrimination

Oppression can be defined as a disregard of basic human rights through degrading or inhuman treatment of individuals or groups. This results in hardship and injustice and is the direct result of an imbalance of power between individuals or groups. Discrimination can be defined as one person treating someone less favourably than they would treat someone else on the basis of colour, race, gender, ethnicity or religious belief.

Smyth (1989) identifies five levels where discrimination occurs, and the practices and effects which are associated with each level.

1 Cultural. People have stereotypes and myths about cultures which are different from their own. These are represented in the media or traditions and customs.
2 Institutional. The legal, educational and health systems fail to consider the rights of different ethnic minority groups. The equal opportunities and race relations legislation opposes all discrimination.
3 Collective. Local communities have sanctions which exclude others.
4 Interpersonal. In contact with other people, the ideas about other groups are confronted or confirmed. Alternatively, certain groups of people may avoid contact with particular groups.
5 Personal. This involves how you feel about yourself and your personal experience and is reflected in your self-presentation and self-image. Methods of dealing with experiences of discrimination at this level would involve building up your self-esteem and re-assessing expectations of yourself.

This model has the potential to allow individuals to begin to examine where discriminatory practices exist in their organizations, or at a personal level.

Empowerment means recognizing the essential differences between people on the basis of ethnicity, disability or gender and ensuring that needs are addressed and met within an acceptable and appropriate personal and cultural context. Equality means treating everyone the same irrespective of individual or cultural differences.

Resources for promoting empowerment and equality

On a more practical note, the work of the Children's Legal Centre in London and the development of the Kidscape programme is at the forefront of developments.

The Children's Legal Centre publishes a monthly bulletin 'Childright' and campaigns on behalf of children's rights. The organization monitors current legislation and policy as it affects children and issues related to health and safety.

Kidscape (at 82 Brook Street, London W1 1YG) is an organization which was developed in the United Kingdom by Michelle Elliott. Now established as a charity, it promotes strategies for children to keep themselves safe. Its emphasis is on 'Good Sense Defence' for young children but its under-fives programme is limited to the age range of three to five years.

The organization aims to encourage children to become more assertive and not to be frightened to say 'no' to adults or other children who are causing them distress. It also teaches children that for their own safety they may have to do things they would not normally be allowed to do, such as screaming, biting or kicking. The programme has been particularly influential in teaching children to protect themselves against bullying. The value of such training tools cannot be overestimated. The material has been tried and tested for its audience appeal and a comprehensive training manual accompanies the package.

Teaching self-protection is based on the empowerment of children because it involves explaining to them that they have rights and enables them to have the self-esteem and confidence to refuse to obey adults unquestioningly.

One effect of this is that we, as adults, may find that our ways of treating children have revolved around petty rules which have no real justification.

Ways of promoting empowerment and equality

Chapter 2 considered ways in which adults could promote children's self esteem. Research has shown that from an early age children are aware of differences in physical appearance such as skin colour. Children soon begin to attribute values to these differences: for example, a person with dark skin may be seen as less important – or has an inferior lifestyle – than someone with light-coloured skin. Children learn their values from adults and these values are conveyed in adults' attitudes and assumptions. A crucial starting point in promoting equality has to be the value-base which adults promote in their child-care practice.

The following statements make up just such a value-base.

- Each child is a unique human being and differences should be respected and appreciated in a positive way.
- Each child has a valuable contribution to make and has the right to be treated kindly and fairly by all.
- Children have the right to privacy and their own belongings and personal space.
- All children and young people should be involved in making decisions about matters which affect their lives.
- All children should have full knowledge of their rights.
- All children should have the right to choose who they want/do not want to have contact with.
- A child's own views and wishes should be explored using non-verbal and verbal methods of communication ensuring the child's voice is heard and expressed.

Anti-discriminatory practice challenges discrimination on a personal and structural level (see Smyth's classification) and involves an active participation in recognizing essential differences between people and speaking out when needs are not being met. Few of us would feel we have the ability or the capacity to change or challenge the institutional or structural basis of discrimination. However, it is possible to examine your own practices, value-base and attitudes. In this way, personal awareness or change in practice can have an effect on others.

Showing respect for children

1 Do you remember children's names?
2 Do you introduce yourself to children?

3 Do you give equal time to all the children in your care?
4 Do you listen to the children in your care?
5 Do you make judgements about a particular child on the basis of class, ability, gender, ethnic origin or religious beliefs?
6 Do you criticize a child or jump to conclusions about their behaviour before getting their explanations?
7 Do you interrupt children or talk over them, not allowing them to be heard fully?
8 How do you show children in your care that they are worthwhile, valuable and important?

Developing empathy with children

1 Can you see the world from a child's perspective?
2 In what ways do you show children in your care that you are an approachable person who will listen to them?
3 Are you alert to the cues that children give about their feelings?
4 How willing are you to pick up and respond to these cues in a way which enables a child to feel you understand what they are trying to say?

Key questions

Use these questions to check back over the material covered in this chapter and assess your grasp of it, before moving on. Discuss the questions, and responses to them, with colleagues and tutors.

- What is meant by children's rights?
- What are the main arguments in favour of children's rights?
- In what ways can empowerment for children be promoted?

Relevant S/NVQ Units

The material in this chapter will help with preparation for the following Child Care and Education S/NVQ Units: C15, P2, C4 and C5.

Further reading

Elliott, M. (1986) *Keeping Safe: A Practical Guide to Talking with Children*, (Coronet Edition), London: Hodder and Stoughton. An excellent read dealing with self-protection and providing an introduction to exercises.

Elliott, M. (1989) *Dealing with Child Abuse: The Kidscape Training Guide*, London: Kidscape Ltd. Training material which replicates the Kidscape methods and offers activities which can be used for one- to three-day courses – an invaluable 'how to do it' manual.

Elliott, M. (1988) *Under Fives Programme*, London: Kidscape Ltd. Part of the Kidscape kit with material for planning and teaching good self defence to children but is limited to 3–5 age range.

Freeman, M. D. A. (1983) *The Rights and Wrongs of Children*, London and Dover: Frances Pinter. A fascinating book which deals with theoretical exploration of Freeman's own liberationist view of children's rights. The sort of book you could dip into and only cover chapters 1 and 3 for your main thesis.

Ways of empowering children

Organization
This activity – and each of the following activities – is designed to enable workers to look at ways in which children's rights can be recognized and promoted.

1 Familiarize yourself with commercially produced material on protecting children; for example, Kidscape material.
2 List the difficulties involved in implementing a programme in your workplace; for example, parental resistance, lack of skills for running a group.
3 Work through the list, identifying strategies to overcome them.
4 Discuss realistic ways of using the material and carry this through.
5 Record what you learned from each session and review the experience on completion.

Activity

Implementing change in practice

1 In pairs, discuss your views on the 'child liberationist' perspective, identifying ways in which you presently have power over children in your workplace (for example, deciding activities they will do).
2 Select one or two ways you think could be altered to allow children some say in what happens.
3 Carry out these changes and record what you have learned.

Activity

Educating others about children's rights

Design a poster about children's rights and organize an opportunity for an exhibition, either by the group itself or on tour around various workplaces.

Activity

Empowering children to have a voice

Encourage the children in your workplace to make a collage with the theme of children's rights. Display the collage in a prominent place and acknowledge the children's contributions by taking individual photographs which can be displayed alongside the collage.

Activity

Respecting children

This activity is designed to enable workers to examine ways of improving practices in their workplace.

1 As a group, brainstorm ideas about how people show respect for each other. Draw up a common list.
2 List ways in which adults can show respect to children.

3 Compare and contrast the two lists.
4 Discuss how practices in your workplace reinforce or deny children's rights and self-respect.

Challenging barriers to empowerment

This activity is also designed to enable workers to examine ways of improving practices in their workplace.

1 Divide into small groups. Using the following list of attributes, each group should write out cards for each one. You may wish to make cards for additional qualities.

Attribute List			
shy	precocious	sociable	faddy
crafty	seductive	boastful	vulnerable
facetious	amiable	wise	humorous
powerful	capable	patient	demanding
argumentative	spontaneous	manipulative	
moody	reserved	trusting	

2 As you deal out each card, the group has to decide whether it agrees, disagrees or cannot agree whether they are attributes which may be used to describe children. (Put to one side attributes about which there is disagreement.)
3 Discuss how these attributes reflect people's personal attitudes and the values they hold about children and how they are used to label children.
4 Contrast how these attributes and their characteristics are used to describe children with how they are used to describe adults. How does this comparison show the ways in which adults create barriers to children's empowerment?

References

Ainsworth M.D.S., Blehar, M.C., Waters, E. and Wall, S. (1978) *Patterns of Attachment*, New Jersey: Lawrence Erlbaum Associates.

Allport, Gordon W. (1955) *Becoming*, USA: Yale University Press.

Archard, D. (1993) *Children, Rights and Childhood*, London: Routledge.

Archer, J. (1992) 'Childhood gender role: social context and organization', in McGurk, H. (ed.) *Childhood Social Development*, East Hove, Sussex: Lawrence Erlbaum Associates, pp. 31–61.

Baumrind, D. (1971) 'Current patterns of parental authority' in *Developmental Psychology Monograph*, 1971, 4(1[2]).

Bowlby, J. (1951) *Maternal Care and Mental Health*, Geneva: World Health Organization.

Bowlby, J. (1953) *Child Care and the Growth of Love*, Harmondsworth: Pelican, 2nd edition, 1965.

Bowlby, J. (1979) *The Making and Breaking of Affectional Bonds*, London: Tavistock.

The Attachment and Loss trilogy:

Bowlby, J. (1969) *Attachment*, London: Hogarth Press.

Bowlby, J. (1975) *Separation: Anxiety and Anger*, London: Hogarth Press.

Bowlby, J. (1980) *Loss: Sadness and Depression*, London: Hogarth Press.

Bremner, J.G. (1988) *Infancy*, Oxford: Basil Blackwell.

Bruner, J.S. (1975) 'The ontogenesis of speech acts' in *Journal of Child Language*, 2, 1–19.

Bull, N.J. (1969) *Moral Judgement from Childhood to Adolescence*, London: Routledge & Kegan Paul.

Butler-Sloss, E. (1988) *Report of the Inquiry into Child Abuse in Cleveland*, London: HMSO.

Clarke, Ann M. and Clarke, A.D.B. (1976) *Early experience: Myth and Evidence*, London: Open Books.

Daines, R., Lyon, K., Parsloe, P. (1990) *Aiming for Partnership*, Ilford: Barnados Practice Paper.

Department of Health (1991) *Working Together under the Children Act 1989: A Guide to Arrangements for Inter-agency Cooperation for the Protection of Children from Abuse*, London: HMSO.

Department of Health (1991) *Patterns and Outcomes in Child Placement: Messages from Current Research and their Implications*, London: HMSO.

Department of Health and Social Services (1993) *Children (Northern Ireland) Order 1993*. Part II Articles 5–7. Draft Statutory Instruments, Belfast: HMSO.

Dingwall, R., Eekelaar, J.M. and Murray, J. (1983) *The Protection of Children: State Intervention and Family Life*, London: Blackwell.

Fahlberg, U. (1985) *Helping Children When They Must Move*, Practice Series 6. London: BAAF.

Garvey, C. (1977) *Play*, London: Fontana.

Garvey, C. (1984) *Children's Talk*, London: Fontana.

Harlow, H.F. and Harlow, M.K. (1969) 'Effects of mother-infant relationships on rhesus monkey behaviours' in Foss, B.M. (ed.) *Determinants of Infant Behaviour IV*, London: Methuen.

Hartup, W.W. (1992) 'Friendships and their developmental significance' in McGurk, H. (ed.) *Childhood Social Development: Contemporary Perspectives*, Hove: Lawrence Erlbaum Associates.

Howes, C. (1989) 'Peer interactions of young children', *Monographs of the Society for Research in Child Development*, 53 (Serial No. 217).

Houghton, D.M. (1988) 'Hypnosis with anxious schoolchildren', in Heap, M. (ed.) *Hypnosis: Current Clinical, Experimental and Forensic Practices*, London: Croom Helm.

Hughes, W.H., Patterson, W.J. and Whalley, H.J. (1986) *Report of the Committee of Enquiry into Children's Homes and Hostels*, Belfast: Department of Health and Social Services.

Huston, A.C. (1983) 'Sex-typing' in Hetherington, E.M. (ed.) and Mussen, P.H. (series ed.) *Handbook of Child Psychology, Volume 4, Socialization, Personality and Social Development*, New York: Wiley, pp. 386–467.

Kohlberg, L. (1971) 'From is to ought' in Mischel, T. (ed.) *Cognitive Development and Epistemology*, New York: Academic Press.

Levy, A. and Kahan, B. (1991) *The Pindown Experience and the Protection of Children: A Report of the Staffordshire Child-Care Inquiry*, Staffordshire: Staffordshire County Council.

Maccoby, E.E. and Martin, J.A. (1983) 'Socialization in the context of the family: parent–child interaction' in Hetherington, E.M. (ed.) and Mussen, P.H. (series ed.) *Handbook of Child Psychology Volume 4: Socialization, Personality and Social Development*, New York: Wiley, pp. 1–101.

Matterson, E. (1989) *Play with a Purpose for Under-Sevens*, Harmondsworth, Middlesex: Penguin.

Meadows, S. (1986) *Understanding Child Development*, London: Hutchinson.

Miller, L.C., Barrett, C.L. and Hampe, E. (1974) 'Phobias of childhood in a prescientific era' in Davids, A. (ed.) *Child Personality and Psychopathology: Current Topics*, New York: Wiley.

Mrazek, D. and Mrazek, P. (1985) 'Child Maltreatment' in Rutter, M. and Hersov, L. (eds) *Child and Adolescent Psychiatry: Modern Approaches*, London: Blackwell Scientific Publications.

Morgan, P. (1975) *Child Care: Sense and Fable*, London: Temple Smith.

Ollendick, T.H., Yule, W. and Ollier, K. (1991) 'Fears in British children and their relationship to manifest anxiety and depression' in *Journal of Child Psychology and Psychiatry*, 32(2), pp. 321–331.

Parton, P. (1985) *The Politics of Child Abuse*, London: Macmillan.

Patterson, G.R., Littman, R.A. and Bricker, W. (1967) 'Assertive behaviour in children: A step towards a theory of aggression' *Monographs of the Society for*

Research in Child Development, 32 (Serial No. 113).
Payne, M. (1982) *Working in Teams*, London: BASW and Macmillan.
Piaget, J. (1932) *The Moral Judgment of the Child*, London: Kegan Paul.
Pugh, G. and de'Ath, E. (1989) 'Parenting in the 1980s' in Stainton-Rogers, W., Hevey, D. and Ash, E. (eds) *Child Abuse and Neglect: Facing the Challenge*, Milton Keynes: Open University Press.
Rutter, M. (1981) *Maternal Deprivation Reassessed*, Harmondsworth: Penguin.
Rutter, M. (1971) 'Parent-child separation: psychological effects on the children' in *Journal of Child Psychology and Psychiatry*, 12, pp. 233–60.
Schaffer, H.R. (1981) 'Social development in early childhood' in Fontana, D. (ed.) *Psychology for Teachers*, London: British Psychological Society and Macmillan.
Schaffer, H.R. (1989) 'Early social development' in Slater, A. and Bremner, J.G. (eds) *Infant Development*, Hove: Lawrence Erlbaum Associates, pp. 189–210.
Schaffer, H.R. (1992) 'Joint Involvement Episodes as context for development' in McGurk, H. (ed.) *Childhood Social Development: Contemporary Perspectives*, Hove: Lawrence Erlbaum Associates, pp. 99–129.
Schaffer, H.R. and Emmerson, P.E. (1964) 'The development of social attachments in infancy' in *Monographs of the Society for Research in Child Development*, 29 (94).
Shepherd, M., Oppenheim, B. and Mitchell, S. (1971) *Childhood Behaviour and Mental Health*, London: University of London Press.
Sluckin, W. (1970) *Early Learning in Man and Animal*, London: Allen and Unwin.
Smyth, M., Schlindwein, H.E.M. and Michael, G. (1993) *Aspects of Implementing Anti-discriminatory Practice in Social Work Education in Northern Ireland: A Preliminary Study*, Londonderry: PIP Printing.
Thompson, N. (1993) *Anti-discriminatory Practice*, London: Macmillan.
Tizard, Barbara (1977) *Adoption: A Second Chance*, London: Open Books.
Woolfendale, S. (1989) *Parental Involvement: Developing Networks between School, Home and Community*, London: Cassell.

Index

abuse 113–122
  'battered child syndrome' 115
  categories 116–17
  causes, theories 117–18
  definitions 116
  emotional abuse, indicators of 120
  historical background 113–15
  neglect, indicators of 119–20
  parent–child relationships 96
  physical abuse, indicators of 119–20
  play, behaviour in 85–6
  protection, guidelines 121–2
  recognition of problem 115
  sexual abuse, indicators of 120
  society's attitudes 114
  special needs, children with 120–1
  state intervention 114
  touching, reaction to 67
activities for students 10, 16–18, 24–6, 34–5, 42–4, 52–3, 61–2, 70–71, 81, 92–3, 102–4, 111–12, 123, 131–2
aggressive behaviour 45–52
  causes 45–6
  changing behaviour 50–1
  circumstances promoting 48–9
  class 48
  family therapy 51
  learned behaviour 46–7
  levels, differing 47
  management 49–51
  physical punishment 48
  reinforcement 46–7
  television, effects of 48
Ainsworth, Mary 5–7
  questions about 7
animals, observation of 2–3, 4
  imprinting 2
  sensitive periods 3
anxieties 36–41
  alleviation and management 40–1
  anxiety disorders 39
  common fears 36
  origins of 39–40
  phobias and panic reactions 38–9
  physical signs 37
  psychological signs 37
  specialist help 38–9, 40
assessment *see* monitoring progress

Bowlby, John 2–5
  criticisms 4–5
Bulger, James 48

Child Protection Register 116
Children Act (1989) 95, 114
  child protection 122
  definitions 122
Children (Northern Ireland) Order (1993) 95, 122
Children's Legal Centre 128
Cleveland Inquiry 115
communication, effective 63–70
  adults' manner 68
  child's ability to understand 63–4, 69
  emotional history 67–8
  hearing 65
  level of development 67
  movement 66
  music 65
  reasons for communicating 68–9
  seeing 64–5
  smelling 66–7
  taste 67
  touch 65–6, 67

discrimination
  definition 129
  see also gender awareness

empowerment and equality 124–30

resources 128–9
ways of promoting 129–30
equality *see* empowerment and equality

fears *see* anxieties

gender awareness 19–24
behaviour 20
discrimination 23
education 22
gender role, learning 19–20
influences 21
media influence 22–3
promotion of 23
stereotypes 20

infants
adoptive parents 8
attachment behaviours 5–9, 11
bonding 1–2, 3–4
communication 64
cultural differences 5
family relationships 8
growth, influences on 8–9
infantile autism 88–9
non-verbal information 13
parents' sensitivity towards 5–6
reactions 6
security 6
self-awareness 12–13
separation from parent 7–8
siblings 8
socialization 27–8

Kidscape 128

language
hearing loss 89
impairment 89–90
speech problems 90
local authorities, duties of 96

monitoring progress 72–80
confidentiality, policy on 79
forms of records 72
methods 74–6
normality, measurement 77–8
relative normality 78–9
reliability 76–7
techniques 73–4
types of information required 72–3
validity 77

moral understanding *see* right and wrong, awareness of

neglect *see* abuse

observation *see* monitoring progress
oppression, definition 128

parenting 96–8
birth parent 96
legal parent 96
parenting parent 97
support *see* partnership with parents
parents, partnership with *see* partnership with parents
parents, relationship with 1–9
adoptive parents 7
attachment behaviours 5–7
bonding 1–2, 3–4
cultural differences 5
deprivation 3
growth 8–9
security 6
sensitivity 5–7
separation 4, 7
partnership with parents 94–102
anti-sexist practice 101–2
areas of support 97
barriers 94, 100–1
development 98
implications 94
legislative context 95
parental involvement 98–100
parental responsibilities 95
parents' confidence 101
power imbalance 100
pre-school caring 98
staff's skill and attitudes 101
phobias *see* anxieties
physical abuse *see* abuse
play 82–91
abused children 85–6
aggressive children 85
behaviour, deviance 83–4
brain damaged children 86
development disorders 87–9
environment for diagnostic purposes 90–91
hyperactive children 86–7
infantile autism 88–9
inhibited children 84
language impairment 89–90

participation 83
value 82
Plowden Report (1967) 98
Poor Law Amendment Act (1889) 114
possessions *see* self-identity, ego-extension
Prevention of Cruelty to Children Act (1904) 114
Prevention of Cruelty to and Protection of Children Act (1889) 114
protection of children *see* abuse

questions for students 9, 16, 24, 34, 41, 51, 60, 70, 80, 92, 102, 110, 122, 130

recording *see* monitoring progress
right and wrong, awareness of 54–60
adults' lack of discussion 57
development 54–6, 56–7
different types of rules 58–9
growing awareness of others 58
justice, ideas of 56
moral autonomy 59–60
moral rules, unchanging 59
obedience 55
obeying the rules 56–7, 58
rights of children 124–30
extreme view 125
moderate view 125
UN Convention on the Rights of the Child 127

S/NVQs 9, 16, 24, 34, 41, 51, 61, 70, 80, 92, 102, 110, 122, 130
self-identity, emergence of 11–16
ego-extension 14
expectations of others 13
failures 14
growing independence 11–12
self-concepts, growth of 11–15
self-consistency 15–16
self-esteem 13–14
standards, imposition of 13
sexual abuse *see* abuse
sexual identity *see* gender awareness
socialization 27–33
changes in behaviour 28–9
friendships 32–3
interaction with adults 31, 32
internalized attitudes 29
parental behaviour 30
parental support 31
promoting development 33
relationship with parents 28, 29–30
relationships generally 32
social pressures 29

teams and teamwork 105–10
activities 105–6
assertiveness skills 109
definitions 105
development 106–7
importance 105
leadership style, importance of 107
members' contributions 108–9
networks 105
stress, sources of 109–10

UN Convention on the Rights of the Child 127